ⱯST

THIS BOOK SHOULD BE RETURNED ON OR BEFORE THE LATEST
DATE SHOWN TO ANY LANCASHIRE COUNTY LIBRARY

- 8 OCT 2004
3 0 OCT 2004

SKELMERSDALE

FICTION RESERVE STOCK

AUTHOR	CLASS
REHAK, D.	F

TITLE

A young girl's crimes

County Council

LANCASHIRE
COUNTY LIBRARY
Bowran Street
PRESTON PR1 2UX
LL1   Recycled

A
Young Girl's
Crimes

David Rehak

AmErica House
Baltimore

© 2001 by David Rehak.

Quotations in this work are taken from *Philosophy In The Bedroom* by the Marquis de Sade from the *Oeuvres completes* (16 vol., Paris, 1966-7) and are the author's own translations from the French.

First printing

ISBN: 1-59129-056-2
PUBLISHED BY
AMERICA HOUSE BOOK PUBLISHERS
www.publishamerica.com
Baltimore

Printed in the United States of America

DEDICATED WITH LOVE

to
my parents, Dagmar and Pavel,
to
my good friend, Ryan,
and to
Maude Langlois,
ma Venus noire, ma Gisele d'Estoc, mon
petit oiseau rouge, ma petite hantise.

I haven't forgotten you, Maudie.

Dedicated to

Rachilde (1860-1953), the first modern
female writer to study the darkest, most
unusual recesses of women's psyche.

Acknowledgements

First and foremost, I'd like to thank my parents for all their support, every kind of support, especially in the last half-dozen years or so. Their faith and understanding have made all the difference in the world; without it I would, literally, not have been able to write half the things I've written. I would not have had the same time or opportunity to.

Secondly, I would like to thank those other writers, editors, professors, etc who throughout the years of my literary development and apprenticeship at one time or another looked at my work and gave me helpful criticism and advice: David Coward, Bill Appel, Richard Lynch, Terence Young, Bill Stenton, John Newton, Joan Rickard, and a few others.

I'd also like to express my gratitude to my fine agent, Brenda Bailey, for her professional expertise and confidence in my writing.

Last but not least, I'd like to thank all my friends and acquaintances from Nanaimo and beyond; past and present. They've helped to shape me into the person I am today. And, of course, my sister Simone, who is someone I can talk to about anything, and with whom I have a close spiritual connection.

Dave Rehak
August 2001
Nanaimo, B.C.

"…I rest in the thought that the moral code is established only for normal human beings, but is not binding for the abnormal. Of course, the human being who is endowed by nature with sentiments of refinement, but whose constitution is abnormal and outside the conventionalities of society, can never be truly happy…

"This is the history of an unhappy woman who, by the fatal caprice of human nature, is deprived of all joy of life and made a victim of sorrow."

–*Psychopathia Sexualis*, R. von Krafft-Ebing

Chapter 1

It was noon and the sun's pale light came down as sharp as a razor, piercing into the eyes of the world. A rabbit scurried through the bushes like a rocket, but other than the wind, as it swept up a debris of leaves from one part of the country to the other, the forest seemed quite undisturbed. Flora was picking wild raspberries, filling them up in her bucket. She loved raspberries. They gave her rashes, but what does a sixteen-year-old care? When her three buckets were overflowing with that ripe, delicious fruit, she headed for home, strolling down the rough, narrow path that led to the garden of her father's stone mansion.

Flora Darby was already mature-looking for her age. Her body showed all the curves of a grown and voluptuous woman. But she was still growing, both in mind and in beauty. Thick, rich, wavy Scottish locks of orange hair matted her head, contrasting exquisitely with her blue-green eyes. Her lips seemed almost naturally crimson, with a tinge of purple. Her nose was small and delicate, like her slender neck. Then there were the smooth, curving buttocks and firm, broad thighs; the soft, moon-shaped bosom, and long, slender legs.

Although at times her behavior appeared to her father to be somewhat unusual, she possessed an intelligent and precocious mind to match those great looks. She had been undergoing a strict and first-rate education since age three thanks to her father, Frank. He was a shortish, stout, neurotic sort of man with a British accent who, though stern and old-fashioned, nevertheless believed in a woman's right to education. He could not tolerate ignorance, or the "incompetent public education system," as he called it. As for the private school system, he knew well from his boyhood days at Eton how frightening and corrupt it could be under the surface. In his view, in-home schooling was the best option. He'd be able to keep a close eye on his daughter, and she would be safe from the luring, dangerous, and "wicked" ways of the outside world. He hoped to keep her in his secluded country mansion forever. Flora had been raised and taught by her tutor, Miss Strachey, a woman in her sixties who shared her father's strict and narrow-minded opinions. She was a cold and impersonal instructor who had tutored Flora's older brother too, when he was younger. He also lived in the many-roomed Victorian mansion, which stood so tall and forbidding, like some old haunted house. The only thing that really bothered Flora was that she didn't know anybody outside of the mansion and had no friends. There wasn't another house for miles, as her father owned all of the two hundred acres surrounding the mansion. The land was all nature, mostly forest and pasture. Flora was free to go anywhere, and yet, she could go nowhere.

The year was 1972: summer; the place: western Alberta, Canada.

"Flora!" came the voice of Miss Strachey as the young girl was walking down the path with her small buckets. "Time for lunch!"

"Coming!"

Flora hurried through the spacious, blooming garden to

the patio, where the food was being served. There she was met, as usual, by her father, who was too wealthy to work. All those millions he'd inherited after the death of his own father! And her brother, Bill, joined them also. He took after Frank in many ways, idle as a piece of rotting wood. He liked to go hunting, which Flora strongly disapproved of. Killing all those defenseless creatures for nothing, she thought.

Bill was six years older than Flora, and just as smart and attractive-looking as she was, with his dark-blonde hair, sharp blue eyes, and muscular physique. But unlike Flora, he was obsessed with his body, working out at least four hours a day. His whole nature was obsessive. He had his own weight room. People said he looked a lot like his mother, but the tragic thing was, their mother had died in an automobile accident when he and his sister were still very young. And that was one of the main reasons why Frank was so eccentrically over-protective about his kids, especially the younger Flora. It would have killed him even to lose one of them. Frank kept it a deep and dark secret that he was clinically neurotic, something he'd been aware of since it was diagnosed in his youth that he had inherited a severely tainted genetic pool from his mother. The doctors had warned him that bad heredity might very possibly be passed on to his children. He laughed off such a suggestion. And all his life, he did all he could to hide and suppress any "abnormal" psychological traits his behavior might otherwise disclose.

"So, what have you done with yourself today, my beautiful daughter?" said Frank half-interestedly.

"Oh, nothing, as usual. I picked stupid raspberries. Now my hands are all sticky and stained."

Frank frowned; "Go wash them."

"Look how big my muscles are now," said Bill, sticking his bulging, well-formed bicep in Flora's face.

"You're such a show-off," spat Flora, pretending to ignore him. She was very fond of him, but didn't like to show it. "You didn't shoot any animals today, did you?"

"No... But I shot a squirrel's tail off! Ya shoulda seen that sucker move!"

"You're cruel! Dad, did you hear what he just said?"

"Yes, darling. But you can't believe everything your brother tells you."

More calmly, she said, "Did you or didn't you do that?"

"Am I under oath?"

"Yes!"

"Well, then, in that case, I didn't."

"Swear?"

"Ya. I'd have the tail with me as a souvenir if I did, wouldn't I?"

"Okay, I believe you."

The truth of the matter was that Flora loved animals, just as she loved the wonders and beauty of nature unhampered and unspoiled by the industrial hand of Man. And she couldn't bear the thought of them suffering.

By the time the meal was over, Flora was already terribly bored. "It's always so quiet here. Nothing ever happens. Why can't we live in the city?"

"But you love the countryside," said Frank.

"Of course... but there's nobody here to be friends with. I'm all alone. I–"

"Now, Flora, you know we've had this discussion a thousand times. I've warned you time and time again about life in the real world. It's a harsh place, especially for a young girl like you. When you're an adult, and a part of that world, you'll know exactly what I mean."

"Okay, okay. But I'd still love to go to a boarding-school, or even a convent-school… anywhere where I can be with people my own age… If I live this way any longer, I fear I might forget what it is to be human. Is it really natural, such a sheltered life for a teenage girl?"

"Perfectly natural. I mean, look at your brother and how well he turned out. He grew up the exact same way."

"But he has things to do. He has his hunting and exercise to keep him occupied! What do I have?"

With those words, she left the table in a hurry, crying. She ran into the house and up the stairs, slamming her bedroom door behind her.

Her father and brother only laughed.

"Poor child, these teenage years are definitely the hardest. Especially for girls. But does she always have to get so hysterical? Doesn't she know it's not the end of the world? But at least we know where she gets her fire from. Her mother. Now that woman could really throw a fit!" As if realizing his remark to be indelicate, Frank added, "What a woman your mother was! God rest her soul!"

"I don't mean to contradict you, Dad, but it's YOU she gets her so-called 'fire' from," said Bill with a chuckle.

Frank gave him a grim look.

Chapter 2

Flora didn't take breakfast the next day. She skipped lunch too.

"What's wrong with your sister?"

"I don't know," said Bill to his father as they ate their lunch. "Should I go check up on her? Who knows, something might've happened to her."

"No," said Frank, biting into a ham sandwich. "But she's probably still upset from yesterday. I wouldn't be surprised if she's done something foolish... Go up and see."

Bill excused himself and went up to her room. She wasn't there. He started to get worried. Where else could she be, he thought, searching the other rooms where she could often be found. But not a trace of her. Had she sneaked out of the house? Was she hiding somewhere?

Just as he was about to tell his father about her disappearance, Bill heard what sounded like the page of a book turning. It came from the library. Upon entering it, he found Flora sitting at a chair, intently reading away. This was unusual for Bill. He'd never seen his sister pick up a book in his life.

"What are you doing?"

"What does it look like I'm doing," she said rudely, her face grimacing with disgust before resuming its former look of interest as she started reading again. She still appeared to be angry.

"Well... we've been worried about you, that's all."

"I've taken up reading. It's actually a lot better than I expected. I think school-work turns kids away from reading. We should be able to read what WE want, not what teachers assign to us."

Bill, who had been an avid reader all his life, quickly snatched the book from her grasp.

He read its title out loud: "*Philosophy In The Bedroom* by the Marquis de Sade... Is it any good? I've never heard of this author."

Flora cried out: "Give it back! Give it back!" It was as if a dark secret were about to unfold to her great dismay.

Bill's curiosity about the book only grew when he saw her reaction. Flipping through the volume, he dropped it after reading for a moment here and there. Shock filled his being.

"Where did you get this filth?"

Flora didn't say anything and Bill could see she was seized with guilt.

"I asked you a question. Where'd you get it? Certainly not from father's library."

"Where else? I was bored. I was snooping around in here when I discovered it hidden behind that book-shelf over there." She pointed.

"I can't believe this. And all our lives, dad's been lecturing us on sexual morality and all that kind of stuff! And all the while, he's been collecting pornography. What hypocrisy!" Realizing that he might be exaggerating and believing that a son shouldn't talk about his father in that way, he added in a milder tone: "Well, I don't know if he's been collecting pornography. I mean, I've read most of these books and I haven't found any."

13

"Who knows. He could have it locked away somewhere for all we know."

"It's best if we just keep quiet about this, okay? Got it?"

"Sure," said Flora indifferently.

"Now put the book back exactly where you found it."

Chapter 3

Flora began to devour the Marquis de Sade. In the past, she'd never seen or read anything even remotely obscene. Her father was very strict in that regard. He'd spent his entire life trying to keep any harmful or potentially harmful influences as far away from her mind (and hands) as he could. Everything she'd ever read in the past came directly from the lessons given her by the tutor, Miss Strachey, and had to be approved by her father first. But Flora's sexuality was still budding at her age and this new reading material only made it more intense.

That night, Flora got out of bed when it was all quiet and everyone was asleep. Sliding out through her bedroom doorway, she sneaked off into the library. Her feet felt cold against the hardwood floor of the corridor, until she reached the carpet of the library. She stuck her arm behind the books on the shelves, and after some clever searching, she uncovered three more books by the same infamous author, including the endless and perverse *120 Days of Sodom* and the tragic *Justine*. She also found a key, but she didn't know what for.

Flora's eyes lit up as she examined both volumes. They were very old books, with torn and faded covers. She opened one of them and read something to herself in a whisper; the hero in the novel was talking about a young girl he and his friends had captured:

"...I will implant in this pretty little head the ideals of the lewdest excesses; we shall set her afire with our philosophy, exciting her with our desires... I shall take great joy in this criminal sensuality of teaching lessons and shaping the tastes of the sweet innocent we've caught here in our nets. And, of course, it is obvious that I shall do all that is in my power to pervert her, to destroy and obstruct such false ideas of morality as may already have befuddled her; I desire to make her as wickedly clever, as irreligious, as debauched as I am."

She turned to another page, where the same character was speaking again:

"The more we desire to be aroused, the more we want to experience violent thoughts and feelings."

Flora turned a few more pages:

EUGENIE, touching Dolmance's testicles: Oh! How irritated I am, my friend, with the opposition you take against my desires! ...And these two globes, what is their use, what are they called?

Mme. DE SAINT-ANGE: The word is balls... Testicles is the medical term.

She couldn't believe her eyes and her heart raced when she came across the following:

Ah! scream out, mother, cry aloud as your daughter fucks you! As for you, Dolmance, you're buggering me! ... Here I am then, committing incest, adultery and sodomy all at once, and all this in a girl who has only just been deflowered! ... What progress, my dear friends!

Suddenly, something else caught Flora's eye. Kneeling down, she uncovered a hidden vault in the wall. Taking the key, she jammed it into the lock. It fit. She opened it and was shocked to come upon a little space in which were stored countless sexually explicit photographs, magazines, and books. She went through some of the titles: *Orgies At The Bar*, or *Little Billy's First Trip To The Brothel*. Some of the more noteworthy were *My Secret Life* and *Story of the Eye*. She now saw her father for the pretender that he was – a man who sure didn't practice what he preached.

Through her exposure to the material, Flora's road to erotomania was paved. Her father suspected nothing. They hardly ever saw each other, though they lived under the same roof. Finally she had something to do with her evenings, and she spent them with her "findings" after her late-afternoons in the woods. She was always sure to lock the library door first, of course. Flora's idea of the erotic and of erotic appeal was completely shaped by those crude and scatological writings and pictures, unlike with most other females her own age. While other teenage girls were shyly kissing their boyfriends, she was fantasizing about the darkest outer limits of eroticism.

Her rebel streak, fueled by the recherché sex and violence she was getting into, started to settle in. Her bond with her father became very thin. She resented him strongly for the oppressive power he exercised over her life.

Chapter 4

The months flew by, and before she knew it, Flora was seventeen years old.

While picking mushrooms one day, she saw a young boy about half her age walking aimlessly through the trees, hunching over as if he were exhausted. He wore dirty clothes and his all around appearance was shabby.

"Hey, you there!"

"Me?!"

"Yes, you!" Flora hollered. "What are you doing here? This is private property. You're trespassing!"

"I'm sorry," he said meekly. "I didn't know. I'm... I'm..."

"What's your name?"

"Jamie."

"Where do you live?"

"Nowhere... I mean... I'm an orphan, I ran away from my orphanage. Couldn't stand the god-awful place. I had to get out. All they did was beat ya. And them canes they had... Gosh, I'm glad I'm out!"

Without a word of warning, Flora overwhelmed the boy, picking up a piece of birch.

"That's what you get, you disobedient brat!" hissed Flora, stinging him with firm and unrelenting strikes. "Who said you were allowed to leave the orphanage! You knew this was comin' all along! Little troublemakers like you need to be dealt with quick 'n' proper! I'll bet those poor people who take care of you are worried sick! Ever stop to think of that? Huh?"

The boy didn't reply, only screamed in pain.

When she started getting tired and dizzy, Flora stopped and dropped her instrument of punishment. She couldn't believe what she'd just done. She was in as much astonishment as the boy was in pain.

"Shhh! Shhh! I'm sorry, I'm sorry," she said in a mutter, trying to bring his voice down. "Remember, you mustn't tell, you mustn't tell…" Flora repeated over and over. "I'll help you get where you want to go. Where are you trying to get to anyway?"

He stopped crying after a while and said, "My uncle's house. He's old – twenty-seven! The court said he was an unfit guardian because he drank and gambled and stuff, and they took me away from him. But I want to live with HIM, not in some stupid orphanage!"

Flora sat down beside him. "Do you forgive me?" she said sweetly. Suddenly, she could hear the sound of her father calling.

"Damn it, girl, didn't you hear me calling?" said Frank, eventually finding her with the young boy. "Who's this?"

"Jamie. He's lost," she said. She was still very afraid of her father and his severe authority. Nervously, she mumbled on and finally started to make sense: "He… he got lost trying to find his uncle's house and–"

"All right, all right. We'll take him home."

Knowing nothing about the boy's escape from an orphanage, Frank agreed to take Jamie back to his uncle's house.

"How long have you been living with your uncle?" said Frank as they reached the mansion and went inside. "He's twenty-seven, did you say? Where are your parents?"

"I've been living with him all my life. My folks are dead. It was a car accident. I was only a baby when it happened."

"Hmm. My wife died the same way." Frank sympathized. "Are you sure your uncle can care for you? Wouldn't something like an orphanage or a foster home be a better place?"

"No! No! No! No orphanage! I hate the place! Don't send me back to the orphanage! No, not the orphanage!"

"What's he talking about?" he asked Flora.

She pretended not to know.

"Just calm down!" said Frank. "I'll take you to your uncle. I don't know what all this other stuff is about, but you can sort all that out between yourselves. Just tell me the address. What street does he live on?"

Jamie, recollecting, said, "He lives on Duncan Avenue."

"I know where that is. Come on, I'll take you."

"Okay!" said the boy enthusiastically, jumping up and down. "Thank you! Thank you!"

Jamie had had it in mind to tell Frank about how his daughter abused him, but in the excitement of the moment, overjoyed to soon be re-united with his uncle, he completely forgot about it.

He was given something to eat and immediately driven to his uncle's house.

Chapter 5

Bill and Flora decided to have a walk to the vast and open pasture-lands beyond the forest. The day was cloudy and the air felt chilly on the skin, even when inhaled. It was a sort of long way to walk, but they got there all right.

"Flora, why don't you like father?" Bill said at the foot of the clearing. "I could never understand it. I mean, sure, he has his bad and unpleasant side, but..."

"Isn't it obvious why I don't like him? He's made me his prisoner. He knows how much I want to get away, and yet for some bizarre reason, he keeps me under lock and key."

When they were little, Bill would chase the cows, which made Flora laugh like crazy. Once, though, his foolish, reckless bravery got him in trouble when a billy goat rammed his behind with its horns, sending him flying. Flora then laughed harder than she ever had in her life.

"Let's go feed the horses," said Bill, changing the subject.

And fine horses they were. Two midnight-black steeds with shinning coats, one white, and three brown. They looked eager to be hand-fed, standing there by the fence and leaning over with their necks. The white one was too eager. Flora didn't let go of the grass in time and the horse bit her hand.

"Ouuuuu!"

"Jeez, are you okay?"

"The sucker bit me! Damn, that hurts!"

"Is there a mark?"

Bill tried to rub it better. There was a red imprint from the teeth.

"You're not even bleeding."

"So? It still hurt!" she exclaimed, irritated by his insensitivity.

"Okay, then I'll kiss it better."

And he started kissing her idiotically from her shoulder to the tips of her fingers.

He faked a French accent: "Mon cheri, your arms are so soft and pretty."

Flora giggled. "That tickles! Stop!"

"No, my love, I am under your spell. What can I do?"

She laughed harder, trying to push him away. But at the same time, other feelings were taking root – shameful feelings, forbidden feelings. Flora had always thought her brother was strikingly handsome. But this was actually the first time that he inspired an amorous thought in her.

Suddenly an old man appeared, as if from nowhere. He could have been seen coming, but Flora and Bill were too preoccupied in their silliness to notice. He was an employee of their father's.

"You youngsters better get going now!" said the man in an unpleasant tone. "This is farm country, not a lovers' meeting-place!"

"He's my brother!" shouted Flora.

"Well, that's even worse! This isn't Texas, you know!"

They didn't understand what he meant by that. They left for home.

Suddenly, the sun came out in all its brilliance and

glory. Its shine painted a smile on Flora's lips as she looked up.

Chapter 6

Flora's schooling began every weekday at ten o'clock in the morning, and usually ended at about four. She preferred Miss Strachey to give her her lessons from the patio outside rather than the indoors. Flora very much disliked the prim and proper Miss Strachey, such a mean, spinsterish, domineering woman who often seemed to find such pleasure in humiliating her student and trying to make her feel stupid. One day, Flora decided she'd had just about enough.

Miss Strachey started math, Flora's worst subject. Using a textbook, she gave a few exercises for Flora to do, without first explaining anything.

"You have ten minutes to finish it, so hurry up," Mrs. Stratchey said.

Flora looked at the equations on the page and sighed: "Oh, geometry. I hate geometry."

"Well, go on. Do the work."

"I don't know if I can." She pointed to one of the more daunting equations. "How do you do this one again? I've forgotten the formula for doing this part."

"Oh Christ, girl, there is no formula; it's a simple method, you just simply start with the circumference and–"

"What? You never explained that."

"Every idiot knows that circumference means the area around an object. My God, when will you ever pay

25

attention? How many times must I tell you—"

"You're a horrible teacher!" Flora gasped, for once showing the guts to stand up to her. "You never clarify anything. And you go too fast. I can't keep up! I don't see how anybody could!"

"Oh, and is it my fault you're a simpleton? You probably can't even do the most basic algebra! If you don't try harder, and if you continue this way, I'll have no choice but to fail you. You'll have to repeat this year."

"Just try it!" said Flora, grimacing.

Flora was upset about the incident for the rest of the day. The time had come for her to do something about her tutor, she thought. She waited in her bedroom patiently till it was dark and the old grandfather clock struck twelve.

With the still night air permeating the darkness, Flora tiptoed out of her bedroom, closing the door behind her without making a sound. There was a pillow in her hand.

Like a mouse, she proceeded down the long hallway, and when she got to the door at the very end, which led to Miss Strachey's bedroom, she opened it slowly. The old tutor was sleeping like an angel, or rather, like a hog, with her snotty snores and giant heaving of the chest. Her blanket was tugged up to her neck and her scabby, fleshy, disgusting feet were uncovered. The odor they emitted could have overpowered any pleasant-smelling scent.

Flora closed the door behind her and made her way towards the bed. With both hands, she held the pillow in front of her. Sweat dripped onto it from her own forehead. Her limbs trembled. She was very nervous about what she had come to do.

As she raised the pillow above the woman's head, and

just as she was ready to lower it, an owl cooed from a branch not far from the window, and Miss Strachey awoke, slightly startled by it. Their eyes met, which was an awkward moment for Flora, hastening her to finish her scheme – and finish it quickly. She pulled the pillow down over the woman as hard as she could, putting all of her strength and weight behind it. She could hear the smothered gasps of her victim and they excited her whole body, sending tingles all over.

Flora's desire was unquestionably erotic, but it was also sadistic hatred. This was her sick revenge against the old governess for years and years of domination and humiliation. Now the roles were reversed.

Chapter 7

The murder caused a big local scandal, but since there were no witnesses to the crime, and no apparent suspects, the investigation came up empty-handed. There were no finger-prints either, since Flora had worn latex gloves from her chemistry set, and these gloves were later destroyed.

It didn't take long for Miss Strachey to be replaced. Flora had only one more year of schooling to go, and then she would be free. Free to leave her restricted life at the mansion to enter "the outside world" her father never had a positive word to say about.

When her new tutor arrived, Flora ran downstairs to meet her face to face. She was curious to see what she looked like and was pleasantly surprised. There, in the open front doorway, stood a far younger and better-looking lady than Miss Strachey had been. She was unmarried and in her mid-thirties. She had the most beautifully silky, long, straight, raven-black hair. Her eyes were sensual, and almost seemed to draw her in. Compared to Flora, she was small and petite, but very tall. Her breasts were scrawny and she had a tiny but nicely shaped behind.

Their eyes met and the woman smiled at Flora.

"And you must be Flora!" she said happily.

"Yes," said Flora, shaking hands with her.

"I'm Miss Barrett. You can call me Tiffany."

"Yes, we've been expecting you. Please, come in."

Tiffany was a cheery kind of person, full of humor. And her intellect matched Flora's. She immediately started treating Tiffany like an equal as soon as she became aware of this fact early on. They hit it off from the start and a close friendship developed, more than just your typical teacher-student kind.

"It really is horrible what happened to the last tutor who worked here," Tiffany said casually the following morning. She just blurted it out.

"Yes, I suppose," said Flora. "But she was an old hag anyway. I'm glad I don't have to see her ugly face again."

Tiffany was startled by her student's callousness, but said nothing.

From the very beginning, Tiffany made her views on life, and especially men, known to the impressionable Flora. She made no bones about it – she hated men. She was a self-styled feminist.

"Never forget, Flora – men are scum. All my life, I've been used and abused by them. The worst kind of man," she said, "is the wealthy sexist who thinks he can get any woman, if not by his looks, at least by his bucks. Yes, it didn't take long before I broke off all relations with them, except for my cousin Mat, whom I love like a brother."

In return, Flora introduced her to the writings of de Sade. But the woman was repulsed by them and tried to discourage Flora from her "unhealthy" interest in the Marquis.

"How could you like this? It can't be normal."

Tiffany called Flora down for her lesson. They sat down. It was her second day with her new teacher.

"Okay, now I'm going to give you a short oral exam, just to make sure you have a good grasp of the material we went through yesterday, since you need this knowledge to be able to pass on to the more difficult sections. It's all related in some way."

"All right," said Flora, "I understand."

"Good, so we'll start with this: what is the only geometrical shape whose radius can be determined?"

"A circle or sphere," Flora replied quickly and confidently.

"Yes. Now complete this sentence: the radius is a straight line from the centre of an object to the..."

"Circumference!"

"Yes, right again. You're a quick learner."

"Finally I get all this. And to think, it's all so simple."

"I told you."

"You know, I never thought I'd get through this work. It's all thanks to you."

"Well, you're a smart girl. That makes a lot of difference. It sure makes things easier on me."

Tiffany proved a very able teacher, very good at one-on-one instruction, and Flora learned faster and more efficiently under her tuition than she ever had under Miss Strachey's. And as their friendship became closer, so did their mutual attraction to one another.

Tiffany started taking her out to places, to Frank's great dismay. He didn't like such familiarity between them, nor did he like Flora going to town. He even became jealous of their friendship, a relationship he longed to have with his daughter.

It was a bright Saturday afternoon that they set out for the local town of Longview, driving in Tiffany's car.

"So how do you like my vehicle?"

"It's nice," said Flora, unable to think of anything more substantial to say.

"It's a Ford."

"Oh really."

"Yes. Made by the oldest and still the most reliable car manufacturing company out there," she said with pride.

An hour later, they arrived.

Stepping out of the car, Flora pointed to a woman on the sidewalk selling cotton candy:

"Let's get some," she said.

"Ah, this'll bring back memories," Tiffany said, musing.

So, they proceeded down the street, munching on their extremely sugary-sweet snack. Tiffany led them into a small pet store. Flora was fascinated by the tarantula in one of the terrariums, while Tiffany much rather preferred to see how the innocent little fishies were doing.

"Hey, let's go in here," said Flora once they were back on the street. She grabbed Tiffany's hand and practically dragged her into a gun-shop next door.

"Oh, this doesn't interest me," said Tiffany, shaking her head.

"No wait, it IS interesting."

"Guns are for men, not us."

"I want one," said Flora, staring adoringly at a rifle on the rack.

"Nonsense. The only people who need them are hunters... or criminals!"

They spent the rest of the time strolling through parks and heritage sites. The weather remained pleasant and mild right on into the evening.

When they got back many hours later, Frank barged into his daughter's room. There was anger in his eyes.

"I don't want her taking you to town anymore," he said. "Where do you go anyway?"

"Nowhere!" said Flora. "We go shopping... We browse through the shops. That's all."

"Well... well... I forbid it."

"Why?"

He paused, unable to answer at first. "Because... I'm your father and I say so, that's why!"

"That's no good reason!"

"It's reason enough!"

It was no use. Flora couldn't deal with him.

"I've half a mind already to fire her."

"If you did that, I would hate you forever... Forever and ever!"

Chapter 8

On Flora's eighteenth birthday, Tiffany bought her a bicycle.

Tiffany smiled with apparent delight. "Now we can go riding together."

But Flora was depressed.

"What's the matter?" said Tiffany.

"It's just that... I wish... I wish I had a boyfriend. Isn't that what other girls have in high school? I know it is."

"Oh, cheer up, won't you? You're not missing out on anything. Trust me. Men are no good. I've said it once and I'm sure I'll say it again. Women need to find strength within themselves and from each other. That's where they'll find love and acceptance. Men treat us and each other like animals. Women are different. We have feelings. And we know how to make each other feel special, we know how to make each other feel good far better than men can."

Tiffany walked to the library door, locked it from within, and walked back to the table where Flora sat.

"I'll show you what I mean," she said, coming up from behind Flora and running her fingers through her hair. To Flora's pleasant surprise and bewilderment, Tiffany planted her lips on the side of her neck.

"How's that feel?" she whispered in a sensually husky voice.

Flora giggled, "I don't know. It tickles." But she was

enjoying it.

Tiffany spun Flora's chair around and the girl stood up from it to face her tutor. Lust bewitched her eyes, keeping them half-lidded, as Tiffany put her forefinger on the tip of Flora's nose and slowly slid it down. When it got to her lips, Flora opened them and caught the finger with her tongue, licking it like the shaft of a penis. Tiffany moved that same finger down Flora's top, circling one of her nipples over her clothing and proceeding down to her crotch. She sneaked her hand into Flora's panties and felt her cunt-muscles quiver. It was so warm down there. The pulsing felt like a second heart-beat. Flora tried to thrust her groin up against the hand, making them grind together. By this time, Flora was already panting, with sweat-buds sprouting on her face. Lifting her skirt up over her waist, she sat up on the table and spread her legs.

"Such pretty white panties. You like to show me your panties," said Tiffany.

Flora was very turned-on by those words.

"But what you really want me to see is your pussy. Yes, say it. I want you to say it."

"I w-want to s-sh..." stuttered Flora, not able to complete her sentence.

"Say it, or I'm leaving this very second!"

"I want to show you my – my pussy. Play with my pussy. Touch my burning pussy."

In her actions and words, Flora was getting ideas from the pornography she had addicted herself to.

Tiffany joked aloud: "Ha, ha, that's more like it! I was starting to think you were losing interest."

Tiffany got on her knees and started licking Flora's clearly protruding clitoris while ramming her pink cunt with a forefinger.

"What a small slit for such a big girl," she said. "Your pink little opening is so minute. I'll bet I couldn't fit more than two fingers in here. You pubescent cunt, you! I love young cunts. So fresh and new. You've never been sucked, have you? No, of course not."

Flora's sex-lips were short and almost invisible. Her pussy-pouch was plump, covered with a thick carpet of red and light-red hair.

Soon the sweet nectar began to leak and Tiffany was ravenous about not missing a drop. After Flora experienced her climax, they changed positions.

A few step-by-step instructions and some real hands-on training followed; Flora became a very knowledgeable and talented cunt-sucker in no time.

"Doing this is better than anything I've ever done," the teenager said gigglishly, wildly swinging her head and tongue up and down, side to side, starving for that delicious, juicy cunt-meat.

Tiffany's twat in comparison was very different. The lips of her sex were purplish, loose, wavy, and hung long and low. As for the mons, it wasn't much of a pouch, and the pubis was covered with a sparse growth of hair.

When it was over, Flora still had a few questions.

"What do they call what we just did?"

"Cunnilingus. At least, that's the word used by medical texts I've read on the psychopathology of sex."

"How do you know all this?" said Flora.

"Anything that has to do with Lesbian love, I know."

"Who was the first woman you ever made love to?"

"Some German prostitute when I was vacationing in Europe."

"You didn't mind? I mean, a prostitute?"

"No, not in the least. A cunt's a cunt, right? It could just as easily have been a mother superior for all I cared."

"Why a prostitute?"

"Why not? Well, to tell you the truth, in those days, and it hasn't changed much since then, Lesbian women were hard to come by. And I didn't know where to go meet them. I mean, I heard about them in France and Germany, but it wasn't as though I could ask somebody, 'excuse me, sir, I'm looking for where all the Lesbians get together. I hear there's a thriving homosexual sub-culture and I'd like to take part.'"

They laughed.

Chapter 9

Months passed. Flora and her tutor became lovers. Secret lovers. And Flora made sure that S&M was incorporated into their love-play. Somewhat reluctantly, Tiffany complied with most of Flora's more outlandish sexual demands.

As for Bill, he too was madly in love… with a certain Stephanie Joy – a young woman Frank didn't like in the least. Looking for the right moment to tell his father about his plans to marry her, Bill waited until he was in a good mood, which just happened to be after a great dinner, to announce the happy news. He was in such high spirits.

"Over my dead body!" said Frank. "I told you some time ago to get rid of that low-class goldigger. And now you have the gall to tell me you want to marry the girl? This is too much! What would she have to bring to the marriage? Huh? Answer me this question, if you please."

"Love! Love's value is greater than money!"

"Love? What do you know about love? You ever heard the lyric 'Life is but a dream'? Well, LOVE is but a dream, and dreams eventually end! The euphoria wears off, my boy! Trust a man who's been there! Passion fades. You young people, you're so idealistic! What do you know of the world? Just wait, it'll harden you… If only the freshness of youth possessed the wisdom of old age. How much better off we'd be."

"I don't care what you say. The wedding's already set."

Angrily, Frank shouted, "You get married to that girl and you're no longer my son! I'll disown you, you hear?"

"Good! Good! I don't care! You can keep your filthy unearned millions!"

"Bastard," growled the man, appearing to be gravely insulted. "You don't know how much you'll be regretting those words!"

Chapter 10

The marriage did occur the following week. Immediately after, Bill packed up his things at the mansion, with Stephanie waiting for him in his car.

As he descended down the stairs with two suitcases, the stern figure of his father awaited him at the front door. Frank stood at the doorway, blocking Bill's path.

"Please let me through, father. I'm rather pressed for time."

Reluctantly, Frank stepped aside.

"So you married the slut?"

As if not allowing himself to be shaken by the remark, Bill calmly said: "Yes, I'm fortunate enough to say that Stephanie is now my lawfully wedded wife."

"Disobedient bastard. After all I've done for you. Ungrateful…" muttered Frank, almost foaming at the mouth, murmuring each syllable with an austerity which was far more effective than shouting.

"Father, you know I've always been a good son. Is it my fault you don't want me to marry the woman I love?"

There was a pause.

"Don't you ever attempt to set foot in this house again," said Frank, not even daring to look into his son's eyes for fear that his severity might weaken. "I'm writing you out of the will. You get nothing."

"Thank you, father, thank you," said Bill with sullen sarcasm.

"No. Thank yourself."

As Bill brushed past his father on his way to the car, he turned around for the last time. It was too much for Frank to bear and his eyeballs watered up. But to avoid giving the impression of an oncoming tear, he quickly closed the door behind him. He didn't even get the chance to watch his dearly beloved son as he departed, never to return.

Chapter 11

Flora was shocked at breakfast when she heard what happened. But she wasn't surprised. Father and son had always got on very well, true. But Bill was the type that, if he wanted something, he would go and get it no matter what. What appeared to infuriate Frank as much as anything else was the fact that now Flora would inherit everything. Flora, the daughter who no longer showed him any affection, who didn't love him. What Bill said was true, he really had been a good son to Frank all his life. And now as a reward, not only would he not get one penny from Frank, he was no longer even a member of the family.

Tiffany and Flora decided that the morning was too beautiful to waste indoors and they headed out on their bicycles along the path behind the garden. They made their way into the woods. The eerie, monstrous presence of ancient trees surrounded them from every direction. When Flora looked up, she could hardly see the sky through the green and thickly overgrown branches. The sun's rays shone through the leaves, but only in places. Most of the forest was dim, damp and cool. Silent and solitary.

"Let's go to the pastures, okay?" said Flora.

"Sure. I've never been there."

"They're only about another fifteen minutes away. Shoot, we should've brought some food and things along.

We could've had a picnic."

"What is there at the pastures?" said Tiffany.

"Oh, the animals. The scenery's nice too. It's really private. And you can feed the horses, sheep or cows. They like that."

"Whose land is it?"

"My father's, of course."

They raced their bicycles so that by the time they arrived, they were exhausted. Tiffany was faster and got there first.

"Let's stop here!" said Flora. "I give up. You win."

They sat in some tall grass and leaned against a wooden fence. The distant mooing of cows echoed as if in a valley. Beyond the spacious pastures, a semi-transparent fog covered a whole chain of white-capped mountains.

"Yes, this is a very nice place to get away to," said Tiffany.

"I used to come here all the time... My life was so lonely and pathetic before you came to live with us. Really. I think I'd die if you suddenly decided to leave."

Tiffany chuckled. "I think there's little chance of that happening. Don't you see, my little princess, that I feel exactly the same?"

Flora made a broad smile, squeezing her tutor's hand – a meaningful gesture. "When I graduate, we'll get a place of our own, far away from here."

"Is that what you want?" asked Tiffany.

"Yes."

"Then your wish is my command."

After a few minutes of calm and relaxing quiet in the sun, Flora started to talk: "I could sit here all day, you know. It's not boring at all to observe nature. Your eye is

42

constantly occupied. And if you get tired of looking, you close your eyes, and let your ears take over. Even when there's nearly nothing to hear, it's soothing. It's magic."

"I agree. I like it too. Sure, the city has its charm too. But there's something unique about the country, something you can never capture on any street corner. It's like communion with God or something."

"Tiffany, is there really a God?"

"I suppose we have to believe there is. Not because we fear Hell or want Heaven, but because by believing in God, we laugh uncertainty away. Even if there's only one millionth of a chance that God exists, isn't it better to believe and have at least a tiny hope than not to believe and have absolutely zero hope?"

"I know this will sound silly, but I've always pictured God as a warm hug," said Flora. "I think that comes from a childhood memory of mine. I remember as a little girl when my father read the Bible about how Jesus beckoned his disciples to let the children come to him. He said, 'Let them come, and do not hinder them, for the kingdom of God belongs to such as these.' That moment I felt a force, an energy of the greatest love and peace. I don't know what it was, but it was certainly real. And if somebody had told me I was enfolded in God's arms, I wouldn't have doubted it for a moment... Who would have thought that I'd grow up to do some of the most horrible things you can imagine. Things I dare not mention."

"Like what?"

A pause.

"Won't you tell me?"

"Maybe some day. Not yet. I'm too afraid that I'd lose you."

"Ha, ha. Well, then, we must keep your secret a secret, now mustn't we? What else do you care about, aside from nature?"

"I love animals," Flora said eagerly. "I'm what's popularly being termed 'an animals rights advocate.' What about you? Is there anything in the world that YOU feel strongly about... besides hating wealthy men who treat women as possessions?"

"Ha, ha, of course. Hmm, actually, what I believe most strongly in is self-preservation. You need to have the will to survive. You need the power, intelligence, determination, and confidence to get just what you want out of life, settling for nothing less. In a world dominated by men, this is especially true when applied to us women. And above all, take advantage of promising situations. If money, happiness, or opportunity comes your way, do not let it pass you by."

"Do you really hate men as much as you say?"

"Honey, I'll never be with a man again for as long as there's breath in these lungs."

Suddenly, Flora shrieked as a peal of thunder shook the darkening sky. The bright sun vanished, and almost immediately, a very heavy and abundant rainfall started pounding their heads, drenching them to the bone in a matter of seconds.

"Hurry, let's go home!" said Tiffany. "We'll catch our death out here!"

They quickly got back on their bicycles and started cycling as if in a race against time. The rain was freezing and it came down hard, like hail. The path started getting muddy and it became more and more difficult to ride on the softening terrain. Thunder roared its ear-splitting roars, like the angry voice of Zeus. In all the confusion, Flora didn't notice a hole in the ground ahead, and when her front wheel went over it, she wiped out. The fall was a hard one.

"Tiffany! Tiffany!" Flora screamed.

Tiffany was far ahead and apparently couldn't hear her.

"Tiiifaaanyyy!"

She must have looked back, for she returned, finding a desperate Flora lying on the ground.

"I can't get up!" Flora gasped, touching her sore ankle. "I think I sprained it!"

Tiffany lifted her up, putting the poor girl's arm around her neck and guiding her along. The mansion by then was only another two minutes away on foot.

They finally got back inside safe and sound, but not without much effort. The minute they came in through the front door, Flora's father just happened to be heading up the stairs.

Tiffany called for the maid, who came quickly to assist her with Flora. She looked up at her father. He only gave a momentary glance.

Chapter 12

That evening, the maid was alarmed when she came into Flora's room and found her breathing rapidly and sweating profusely. She was shivering. Flora had been put to bed earlier that day because of the sprained ankle, but the symptoms she was starting to show looked far more alarming than a sprained ankle.

"Dear child, you've caught fever," said the maid, touching the back of her hand to Flora's forehead. "You're hot as a cauldron."

"I don't feel very well."

Tiffany was summoned.

"I'll call a doctor," she said.

Flora started to be afraid. "Is it serious? It's not serious, is it?"

The doctor came shortly after. He was a tall man with a sympathetic voice and German accent named Doctor Swartzer. He gave her a thermometer. A few minutes went by.

"Oh my God, this girl's in danger of losing her life," he said after checking it. "Her temperature is over forty degrees Celsius."

Tiffany explained to the doctor about the awful rainfall from that morning and about the ankle. She looked almost as hysterical and worried as Flora looked sick:

"Save her, doctor. Save her!" she pleaded.

As the doctor gave Flora medicines, the maid got down

by the side of the bed and prayed. She was an old, strong-spirited and wonderfully pious woman.

The temperature went up one degree in the next half-hour.

"She's getting worse," the doctor sighed with increasing despair. "I don't know if her body is strong and healthy enough to make it through such an ordeal. Her immune system is going through one hell of a ride. Let's hope it can sustain the pressure."

Tiffany gasped, "Of course she can! She's tough as nails!"

The injections seemed to help. After another hour, the fever weakened. After two hours, Flora was down to thirty-eight degrees and well out of the danger zone.

"She should be all right by tomorrow morning, or a few days at the latest," said Doctor Swartzer. "Just make sure you watch over her, and make sure she gets her fluids. Give her two aspirins every four hours, just to be on the safe side. If anything should go wrong, you know where to reach me."

"Yes, doctor," said Tiffany, completely relieved.

When the doctor exited the room after a few more encouraging words, he found Frank standing around. The doctor sensed what the man was dying to ask him, so he said, "She's going to be just fine. It was a miraculous recovery."

Frank nodded emotionlessly. He paid the doctor his fee and showed him to the door.

Chapter 13

The doctor's prediction was right. By early next morning, Flora's temperature was back to normal. Tiffany brought her breakfast in bed.

"And how's the Queen this fine morning?"

"Much better." Flora smiled. "Thank you, servant."

"You're welcome, Your Majesty," retorted Tiffany.

Tiffany sat down beside her on the edge of the bed. "You don't know what a scare it gave me last night. I thought maybe I'd lose you."

"You know what I've been thinking about? My brother. It's hard to believe what happened between him and father. They were once so close. I was the one who always felt like the outcast in the family. Like I didn't fit in. Not him. And now it's been so long since I've seen him. We used to get along really well, even though I hated that he liked hunting. And all he ever thought about was his muscles. I wonder what he's doing this very moment."

"Oh, I'm sure he's lying in bed with his beautiful wife, embracing her with those muscular arms of his, and kissing her earlobe," said Tiffany, chuckling.

"I'm almost jealous. There he is, completely free... while I'm stuck here. I swear, Tiff, if it wasn't for you, I'd run away from this place."

"Well, as far as I know, I have no future plans of leaving. That is, if your father doesn't get rid of me."

"Over my dead body!" said Flora.

Chapter 14

Flora's curiosity about her brother increased, and eventually, she called up the operator to get information about his whereabouts. She wanted to keep in contact with him. She was given a number and immediately dialed it.

A woman she didn't recognize picked up the phone.

"Hello, may I speak to Bill?"

"Yes, one moment."

Flora could hear Bill's voice in the background.

"Hello?"

"Hi, it's me."

"Oh, hi sis… It's great hearing from ya. I didn't expect it…"

"Ya, the telephone operator gave me your number. You're obviously not living far away."

"No, not at all. We're just on the outskirts of Calgary. My wife, Stephanie–"

"Oh, is that her name?"

"Ya. Well, anyway, she didn't want to live far away from her family, so we decided to stick around, know what I mean?"

"I'm glad you did," said Flora. "What's Stephanie like? I guess you won't be bringing her around anytime in the near future."

"God, no. I don't plan on coming within a hundred yards of that place as long as he lives."

"Wretched bastard!" came a voice. Flora froze. It was

her father's voice. THEIR father's voice. He must have been listening in on their entire conversation from the other phone in the house. She hung up immediately. She could still hear her father yelling something through the phone at her brother; but all she could make out was, "Don't you dare talk to her again! I forbid it!"

Just as she expected, when Frank got off the phone, he came stomping up the stairs, finding her in the hallway walking back to her bedroom. "Stop!"

She turned around. Not out of fear, but out of bravery. She faced her father with hateful eyes.

"Let what happened to him be a lesson to you. If you speak to that bastard brother of yours again, you'll be out on the street just like him."

"Fine. I'm sure I'd be better off."

A silent rage boiled in each of their faces.

"Why do you hate Bill so much? He's your son! Your flesh and blood!"

"Because he disobeyed me, dishonored me, defied me. It was a spit in the face! Don't you see he brought it upon himself?"

"But why couldn't you accept his marriage? Is it just because she has no money?"

"Not only that. He has the audacity to all of a sudden announce marriage without first even discussing the matter with me… To this day, I've never even personally, officially met the woman! I know next to nothing about her, and all I've seen is a photograph! Did you see how she was dressed in it? I know there were hundreds of women out there better suited to him… and he goes and picks one of the worst choices! How did you expect me to react?"

"But look at the result of your reaction. Are you pleased, really?"

"More pleased than I would be if I had blessed their union!"

Chapter 15

Relations between Flora and Tiffany went well until quite some time later when Flora was nearly nineteen. Flora started sensing a change in her lover, both in the bedroom and out. Tiffany no longer gave herself as she once did. She was drifting away from her. Something was up and Flora didn't know what.

Eventually, she got so fed up that she spoke out: "Why have you been acting so different in the last little while? Is it something I've done? You don't know what you're putting me through. Please, tell me what's the matter."

Tiffany searched painfully for what to say, opening her mouth as if preparing to speak, but then closing it. She had a look about her. A look of guilt. "If I'm hurting you that much, I'll stay silent no longer. I'm sorry, Flora, truly sorry, but the truth is… is… I'm seeing someone. We've been together for the past few weeks."

Every word from Tiffany's mouth was a sword pierced into Flora's heart. Pain and a sense of betrayal overtook Flora. "And all along you never even bothered to tell me?" Her anger was beginning to mount. "Who? Who is she? Who! You know I have a right to know!"

"Actually… it's a he. His name's Richard Powers. He owns a huge car manufacturing plant," she said boastfully.

"It wouldn't be Ford by any chance?" said Flora, sarcastic.

But Tiffany just kept yapping, "He's a millionaire! Don't you see? I'll never have to work again. And I'll get jewels, diamonds, expensive vacations, fancy clothes... he's even promised me a brand new Rolls Royce!"

"But I don't understand! What about all that stuff you said about men being scum, and everything else!"

"Oh honey, I doubt I even knew what I was talking about. I was just jealous of women who were clever enough to latch on to those rich rascals. But now I've got it made. It's easy street from here on in, girlfriend."

"But haven't we forgotten something, Miss Barrett?"

Tiffany appeared to be stung by the formality with which Flora addressed her. "You haven't called me Miss Barrett in ages."

"It's your name, isn't it? Perhaps you've forgotten that your contract binds you here. You can't leave until I complete Twelfth Grade."

"And I don't intend to. You graduate in two months. Then I leave."

Tiffany caressed the girl's cheek. "Please don't be angry with me. Just think of what we had as a pleasant experience that was pleasant while it lasted. Nothing lasts in this world, dear Flora. You'll come to understand... You'll always hold a special place in my heart."

"Bitch!" Flora spat, running into her room and slamming the door behind her.

Chapter 16

Flora did her best to finish her studies and ignore Tiffany outside of the classroom. She thought about having her father fire her immediately, contract or no contract, which was what her desire for revenge craved. But then she realized that she needed Tiffany to get her diploma. Besides, she'd been working for it all her life after all. What was two more months to her?

On the eve she was to graduate and just as she was getting ready for bed, Flora heard the doorbell ring. It was very unusual. Very seldom did they have an outside visitor. And at eight P.M.? Who would think of coming at that hour?

Flora rushed down, and right when she was about to open the door, she saw Tiffany come from behind, all dressed up, with sparkling jewels spun around her neck. Flora opened the door, and there he stood, the man she hated more than she'd ever hated Miss Strachey. And she didn't even know him! But it was his fault that Tiffany had left her embrace for him, or rather, for his wealth.

He and Flora stared at each other blankly. Then, she gave him the dirtiest look, so he was too intimidated to speak.

"Oh, hello," said Flora with false politeness, "You must be the bitch's new boyfriend."

He was a man in his late fifties, but he looked older. Big reddish bulging eyes, lots of hair missing, old wrinkly skin, bushy eye-brows, a crooked beak-like nose. He wasn't very physically attractive at all. In fact, the only thing attractive about him was his bank book. But that was extremely attractive.

Tiffany hurried to greet him, nudging Flora out of the way. "Oh Richard, you look so handsome tonight. I'm ready; let's go. Oh, I just love dancing."

"Well, then you'll like the place I'm taking you to. The best music, the best crowds."

"Great."

"Have a nice time!" said Flora, slamming the door behind them with all her might.

Chapter 17

The day Flora finished her high school studies was the very day Tiffany left. She left with you-know-who, of course, on a fabulous Caribbean cruise. It took Flora no time at all to realize that she was alone again. Emotionally, she'd been alone for the last two months. But now, she was really alone. The boredom and awkwardness of life with a father she had absolutely no relationship with was unbearable. She didn't even take her meals with him at the dinner-table, preferring that the maid bring them up to her room instead.

Flora got so fed up that when she turned nineteen – the legal adult age – she secretly phoned up her brother again and together they arranged her "escape" from the mansion: "No problem. You can live with me and my wife," he said. "I know you two will hit it off."

Flora was overjoyed by the offer:

"Oh thank you, thank you!" She shook with excitement, her head delirious with the promise of freedom.

On the night that followed, exactly five minutes to one o'clock in the morning, Flora left her room as furtively as she had the night she murdered Miss Strachey. She'd put on her best dress and looked quite stunning by any standard.

Cautiously, she proceeded down the stairs, making sure not to make a single creak. She even managed to close the front door behind her without a sound.

The night was a very windy one and the thin, rustling branches of the chestnut tree just outside the maid's window wouldn't stop tapping against it. The maid (Martha was her name) couldn't sleep because of it and she decided to go and open the window, hoping that the irritating tapping would stop as a result.

When she got to the window, sleepy-eyed and sluggish with drowsiness, she saw Flora. She was at the front of the driveway, getting into a car. Bill was in the driver's seat. Martha couldn't believe her eyes and she opened them wide just to make sure she wasn't dreaming. It was no dream.

She opened the window and yelled out:

"Where are you going! Does your father know about this?"

But the car was too far away and the wind too strong to carry the sound of her voice to any distance.

Chapter 18

First thing when he got up for breakfast, Martha told Frank everything that she saw.

"Jesus Christ! And you didn't even wake me up? What the devil were you thinking?"

"I'm sorry, sir... I... I thought you knew... I... I called out to her but there was no answer. I was afraid to wake you up so early. I thought maybe you knew about it..."

"Knew about it? Knew about it? What a stupid woman you are!"

Meekly, on the verge of tears, the maid said: "I'm ever so sorry, sir... I'm only a servant who's good at doing nothin' but what she's told. Damn, I knew I should o' woked you up."

Frank calmed down. "All right, all right, what's done is done. It's all right."

His initial thought was to call the police to drag Flora back home, but then he realized that she was officially an adult, so he had no hold over her anymore, as far as the law was concerned.

Frank stormed through the house like a man who just couldn't stand still. Rage came easily to him. This time, it came as easily as the time his son stood up to him. His mind was hot at work on what his next move would be, when he found a piece of paper slid under the door. It had been put there that night. He picked it up. It said:

Father,

I'm leaving and never coming back.
I find life at the mansion absolute torture.
Don't look for me or try to bring me back.
I'll be living with Bill.

Flora

After Frank read it, he flew into his biggest tantrum yet, throwing furniture all over the place, breaking things, priceless things, as though they were worthless junk. He knew he was powerless to do anything. It was just as he said: what's done is done.

Martha behaved hysterically, like a defenseless woman fearing for her life. She sat on the stairs, weeping madly.

His uncontrollable rage didn't cease until fatigue stopped him. He fell over on the couch, huffing and puffing like a chimney. He lay there for a minute or so, and then quickly sprang again to his feet, heading for his study. Sitting down in his chair, he feverishly started re-writing his last will and testament again. Neither of his children would be his heir. When he was done, he looked like the happiest man in the world. But in a twisted way. Mentally unbalanced.

"Martha!" he shouted, "I'm leaving everything to you! The mansion, my money, and everything else!"

Chapter 19

Her new home was quite a shock to Flora. She was too used to luxury. Bill and Stephanie lived in a rather shabby apartment. One bedroom.

"You'll have to sleep on the couch," said her brother. An ugly, ripped up, worn-out couch.

She took a seat in it. "It sags so low. I can hardly get up."

Bill lowered his head, as if embarrassed. "Well, get used to it. It's the best we have."

When Stephanie came to greet her, Flora decided right away that she didn't like her. Stephanie struck her as very polite, prim and proper. She was also badly dressed.

"How do you do, Flora? Your brother's told me so much about you – really he has, about how much he's missed you, and…"

Stephanie's soft and humble nature didn't bode well with Flora. She saw it as a weakness, as irritating. But she remained courteous and said: "So, you must be Stephanie."

"Call me Steph."

"So, Steph, looks like you'll have to be putting up with me from now on." Flora chuckled. "Sure you won't get annoyed?"

"I'm sure I won't," Stephanie said in her super-sweet, mousy voice. She was a blonde, and she acted like one – the stereotype, that is. On a purely intellectual level, Flora couldn't come close to relating to her. From the very beginning, she felt like being mean and patronizing to Stephanie. And another thing that really bothered her was that Stephanie was physically more attractive than her. Not much more attractive, but more beautiful nonetheless.

"You know you'll have to get a job, though, don't you?" said Bill.

"A job?" said Flora.

"Ya. You've got your diploma. You'll have to contribute equally. We have bills, you know."

"It's okay, though," said Stephanie, "She doesn't have to start working right away. Let her get adjusted first. There's no big hurry." She smiled at Flora, whom she already seemed to be growing fond of.

But in the days that followed, Flora made perfectly clear that she didn't share this same fondness for her brother's wife. And she made no attempt to hide that fact.

"You pig, did you have to drink all the milk?!" said Flora one morning. Showing animosity and starting arguments were her specialty.

Finally, Stephanie just let all of her pent-up emotion burst: "Why do you have to be so cruel? Why do you hate me so much? What've I done?"

Flora kept her composure and, as if ignoring the outburst, replied: "You'd better go and get some milk."

It wasn't long before Flora tried to get Bill to resent Stephanie for their lifestyle: "She lured you away from father's inheritance!" said Flora when Stephanie was taking a bath and they were alone together watching TV.

"Oh, please let's not get into that," he said with a grimace.

"Why not? It's true," she said coolly.

Days later, Bill picked up the local paper on a bright and sunny morning, taking a seat on his couch. It was his day off and nothing in the world was going to bother him. He started reading the articles that interested him, moving from page to page. In a half-hour or so, he was near the end. He had a habit of always finishing off with the obituary column, so he turned to it. Suddenly, his eyes went all big and he lost his breath. He had come upon his father's name! There it was, in print! And there was a brief biographical statement underneath. He couldn't believe it – his father had just died. It came as such a shock because it was so unexpected. Frank had still been in his middle years.

Then, what Flora had said surfaced in Bill's mind. He was lazy by nature and hated work. Through sheer frustration, he became angry: "The mansion and everything could have been mine this very minute. I'd have never had to work another day for the rest of my life. As it is, I have to break my back ten hours a day just to make it from one day to the next!"

Once this resentment for Stephanie was embedded and continued to grow, Flora moved on to the next step in her scheme, which was to seduce Bill. To get him all to herself. The split with Tiffany had left a love-emptiness in her life. And aside from that, Flora was perversely attracted to him.

Stephanie was a waitress and she worked long hours into the night, while Flora was still unemployed. Bill, however, got home from work at about supper-time every evening.

Flora was always very nice to him. She treated him like a king. He started gradually drifting closer and closer to her and farther away from his wife.

One night, he came home, sore and weary from a tough day that had seemed like it would never end. He found the lights off.

"Oh, I'm beat… Where are you, Flora?" he said in the dark.

He flicked on the light switch.

"Here I am, Billy-boy." She chuckled.

She was wearing skimpy see-through lingerie and cute little bunny slippers.

"How do you like it?" she said, seductively trailing her forefinger down along the area between her breasts. "Oooh, it's so cold in here, my nipples are hard."

"Why's it so cold?"

"Because I turned off the heat. Now I want you to come here and make me warm."

"Wouldn't you prefer a blanket?"

"No, I'd prefer you."

She took off the lingerie. It glided off her flesh like a feather. Flora's nakedness confronted Bill head-on. He blushed and looked away, a big grin on his face.

"Flora, what are you doing?"

"I'm trying to tempt you," she said boldly and frankly.

She came right up to him. He was breathing deeply, which she took as a sign of arousal.

"I've been thinking about you all day. Now I'm more aroused than ever. I'm so sick of being a virgin. Can't we have sex? I'm dying to try it."

"We can't… We can't!"

"Why not?"

"For one thing, you're my sister. Besides, I'm married."

"Who has to know? Can't this be our dirty little secret?

I'd like that. I'd like that very much."

"Why me? Seriously. Why me?"

"Do you remember that time when we were younger, when we were at the pastures, and you kept kissing my hand? I never forgot that. I always thought about it afterwards. What could have happened if the old man hadn't come and chased us away?"

"Nothing would have happened."

"You never know."

There was a moment where neither of them seemed to know what to say, so Flora did the one thing she could think of – she kissed him full on the lips. A hard, electric, astonishing kiss. Bill was by no means expecting it, nor did he end it. After a few seconds, he started kissing back. Both of their bodies gave off such passionate body-heat.

"I'm not so cold anymore," Flora said in a deep whisper.

They scrambled into the bedroom, falling hard on the bed, their bodies entangled. They started having a very personal conversation, and Flora got the feeling that she could trust him no matter what. For a long time, she'd had a burning need to confess about the Strachey murder. A deep sense of guilt and remorse were haunting her. She hadn't told Tiffany because she wasn't ready yet to tell anyone. And, looking back, she was glad she didn't tell her. But now, she thought, it was time. It was time to let it out, to release the burden.

"Bill, I have a very big secret to tell you. You must promise to reveal it to no one. You really have to solemnly promise."

"Ya, ya, sure. What is it?" He looked puzzled.

"Do you remember Miss Strachey?"

"Of course. She was my tutor all my life. I can't say I liked her a whole lot, but her murder was shocking. I'll never forget it."

"Bill… it was… it was I who killed 'er. I did it… I hated her."

"No, no, that's impossible. I don't believe you. Why are you making up such a sick story?"

"I'm not making it up! I smothered her. I… I don't want to get too far into it… but –"

Bill backed away from her with a look of utter disgust. He was nauseous to his stomach. "I think I'm going to puke."

Suddenly, Stephanie appeared at the door. When she saw Bill and Flora in the same bed, tears filled her eyes. "You jerk!" she screamed at Bill.

Flora started laughing like she'd just heard the funniest joke in the world.

When he noticed Flora's reaction, Bill was enraged. "You planned this all along, didn't you?! Didn't you?!" He shook her with great violence.

He was right. It had been Flora's hope that Stephanie would find them in bed together and leave him so that she could have him all to herself.

"Stephanie, it really isn't what it seems!" he exclaimed. Then he turned to face Flora. "Just don't come near me! Don't even come near me!"

Stephanie threw all of her clothes any which way into her suitcase and was out the door before Bill could come up with the right things to say.

"Is she gone?" said Flora.

Bill marched back into the bedroom. "You better believe she's gone, you fucking pervert! Now get out!

Out! Out! Out!"

"What? What the hell are you talking about?"

"I want you out of the apartment! You're no longer welcome."

"You can't just kick me out. I want to live here too, you know!"

"You should've thought about that before you walked into my life and messed it all up."

"If there's anything wrong in what we did, you're just as much to blame as me!"

"What we did was wrong. Wrong! It shouldn't have happened... You seduced me! You're the one that's to blame!"

"I don't give a damn about anything you say! And no, I'm not leaving!"

"You don't help pay the rent, therefore you have no right to be here!"

Bill tossed Flora's belongings out the door, and when she wouldn't go, he forcefully tossed her out as well, locking the door.

She pounded on it, begging to be let back in. But it was no use. She got absolutely no answer from him.

Homeless, she left the building and hit the streets – the cold, dark, dangerous city streets. Like some bag lady. Like some tramp. From life in a luxurious mansion to life in the gutter. From riches to rags.

Chapter 20

Bill spent all of his free time fanatically trying to get Stephanie back into his life. It became an obsessive quest for him. He found out that she was again living with her mother and father. It wasn't long before he came knocking on their door.

Stephanie's husky, old father answered. When he saw who it was, he gave a frown and said, "Stephanie doesn't want to see you."

"I'm sure she does, I –"

"No... she doesn't."

If Bill didn't inherit his father's mansion, he certainly inherited his temper. Rudely, he said, "She's my wife! I'm her husband! And she's coming back home with me!"

"Sorry, Bill. Not this time – not ever. And you're not welcome here either... So shove off!"

The door slammed in his face, coming within half an inch of flattening his nose.

Bill knew which her bedroom window was, and he yelled stupidly at the top of his voice, "Stephanie, you're coming home with me now! You hear me? I'm your husband, damn-it!"

The light was on in her room. He could even see her shadowy silhouette behind the curtains.

"I'll be waiting in the car!"

Of course, she never came.

Bill hollered and hollered at her window, his remarks

becoming less and less inhibited as time went on. He was causing a public disturbance and the police was called to take him away.

"You haven't heard the last of me, Steph! Just you remember that!"

Chapter 21

The streets were a wake-up call to Flora. She was forced to beg outside of a bank. But she wasn't pathetic-looking enough to stir really deep sympathy. She still had her nice clothes, her good looks, and so on.

A kind-hearted, somewhat elderly man with curly hair and a bushy beard came up to her. He had very gentle eyes and a very wholesome, sturdy complexion.

"Do you need a home for tonight?"

Flora didn't reply.

"A girl like you shouldn't be out here alone this late. I know you have no home. I can tell. Please let me offer you a place to sleep tonight."

Flora looked up at him. Agony was the story of her whole expression.

"How long have you been out here?"

"All day," she replied. She stood up.

"Follow me," he said, taking her warmly by the hand. Everything about this man seemed angelic, right down to his appearance.

"I live just down the block," he said. "I have an extra bed. You'll be dry and comfortable... How long have you been out on the streets? A month, a year, two years?"

"A day," she said so weakly he thought he heard her wrong.

"What?"

"One day."

He was startled. After some more patient probing, the man got her to open up about her problems with her brother (she left out the more sordid details of the story, of course).

The man's home was a humble little house just on the edge of town, but well-preserved, and with its own distinct little charm.

"You can stay here for as long as you need," he said generously as they entered the doorway. "I've had other run-aways stay with me before in the past. It's nothing new to me."

Though she knew better than to trust a stranger, Flora slept soundly the whole night. The sound of loud motors woke her up the next morning. It was those thousands of cars taking their drivers to work. Slowly, she got out of bed, making her way to the front door.

"Aren't you even going to give me the pleasure of having breakfast with you? Surely you owe me that much." The man who had rescued her from homelessness the night before smiled at her tenderly.

She turned around. "I really should be going, I..."

He started to put on a sad face, exaggerating the expression until Flora began to laugh.

"Please... Please..."

Flora knew she wanted to get some food in her belly first before leaving. "Okay, okay." She smiled back, thankfully adding, "And I just want you to know, I do appreciate all you've done."

"Oh, it's nothing extraordinary. I simply saw a fellow human being in need of help, and was privileged enough to be in the position to take the opportunity. A lesser man would have done the same."

"A lesser man would've taken advantage," said Flora, "and you know what I mean."

"Possibly… yes," he said, pondering for a moment: "We'll always have evil people in the world. How sad it is to realize that the only thing separating human beings from utopia is the one thing we can't do away with – human nature. The application of intelligence and the growth of knowledge, no matter how perfect and refined, is no guarantee for happiness. Life today is proof of that. And all this just strengthens my belief that mankind's moral nature is more important than his mind. Without ethics, society can't function, no matter how sophisticated or advanced it may be. Just imagine if nobody believed in the Ten Commandments. Imagine what tremendous pain and suffering would result, and to what extent! It's horrible even to imagine this. Some of us aren't ethical, but the majority of us are, and that's the only thing that has insured the survival of the human race – the good of the world have always outnumbered the bad. There's only one exception in history – the time before Noah's Flood. And we all know what happened then! Those people were destroyed."

"But did the Flood really occur?" said Flora, taking a seat beside him at the kitchen table.

He handed her some grilled cheese sandwiches and, in reply to her question, said, "Scientists from the secular community have recently discovered what they always denied in the past – a layer of soil deep in the earth's crust indicating that, indeed, a great, earth-consuming flood once occurred at about the time stated in the Genesis account. And it isn't until now, when people are becoming disillusioned with science and technology, that they're even admitting things like this publicly, or the fact that many cities stated in the Bible are today being unearthed by archeologists, thus adding validity to the historicity of the ancient text. Did you know, for example, that at the site most experts say Sodom and Gomorrah once stood, there are rows of pillars of salt, and one single pillar in particular stands alone apart from the rest in a very unlikely spot? Did you know that in the story, Lot's wife was turned into a pillar of salt because she looked back at the city when God had forbidden it? Whew, I could go on for hours... Did you know, for example, that Darwin and Nietzsche's theories are in fact considered much more flawed than they have ever appeared to previous generations? They say it doesn't look like there will be this great 'superman' Nietzsche predicted, and Darwin's 'The Origin of Species' slowly but gradually becomes more and more a hypothesis instead of what it had long been considered – solid scientific fact. Meanwhile, the Bible gains in credibility."

"What do you mean by superman?"

"It was a word the German philosopher Nietzsche coined. Basically, in his theory, the 'will to power' is the biological instinct behind Darwinian evolution and will lead to a 'higher' type of human being, an idealized human being of superior physical and mental attributes far greater than the human being of today. It's a stupid and dangerous belief that led to awful and inhumane experiments in eugenics and even inspired the Nazis in the Second World War."

"So you don't believe there's any credibility at all to the Theory of Evolution?"

"I'll tell you why – because there are just too many uncertainties, too many inconsistencies, too many questions unanswered and subtlely swept under the rug. Why, for instance, haven't they found the Missing Link in the evolutionary ladder yet? If these bones they dig up and call Neanderthal Man and Cro-Magnon Man are indeed primates and not an extinct monkey of some kind, why is it that there is still a great gap in the fossil record?"

Flora found she had much to talk about with him, and was quickly starting to like his personality very much. She found him to be very well-read, and she enjoyed listening to him talk incessantly about his favorite authors.

"Come to think of it though, I don't even know your name!" she said aloud at one point.

"It's John. John Cooper."

"Ya, you do look like a John."

"And what, may I ask, does your typical John look like?"

"A nice man. Like you. A good, decent type."

"That's good to hear," he said, blushing. "Genuine compliments are not the same as flattery. You're right, I most certainly am a John. John to a T."

Though they continued to talk very openly, Flora was careful not to mention her admiration of de Sade and his erotica's great influence over her thoughts and behavior in the past. She didn't want to be judged by him, especially since it was obvious to her that John wasn't a person who would share her admiration.

"Thanks a lot for the breakfast. But I guess I should be off," she said with some regret, having gobbled her last bite.

"Well, you know you're always welcome," John was

quick to point out.

She closed the front door on her way out, feeling sure that she would never see him again.

Chapter 22

Stephanie started her life anew. It was clear that she wanted nothing more to do with Bill, and he knew it. Life with her parents was pleasant enough (not to mention safe and secure) and Stephanie wanted to remain in her new haven at least until she decided what her next move would be. But she was growing more and more afraid, going outside less and less. Bill's car could be seen going by her residence three times a day. Sometimes he even walked past, staring evilly up at her bedroom window as he slowly strolled by. The only time Stephanie left the house was in her parents' company.

However, a reclusive lifestyle didn't suit her. Albeit shy, she was also a social sort of person, and one night her loneliness and depression reached such a pitch that she lingered on the verge of tears.

Stephanie put the leash on her dog and, unbeknownst to her parents, took him out for a walk. She couldn't remember the last time she'd breathed the fresh coolness of midnight air. The neighborhood was as quiet as on any typical Sunday night. Her cute shaggy little dog was also more than happy to get out of the house. As she walked down the suburban sidewalk, she felt a peace and quiet that couldn't be found in the heart of the city, where Bill lived. For once in a long time, she felt a complete freedom from Bill, that he was far, far away.

Suddenly, she could hear footsteps. She looked behind

her. It was a young, very thin boy, no older than fifteen. He looked stoned, like someone on heroin. Stephanie ignored him. When she looked over her shoulder a second time, she saw him disappear into the bushes, falling to the ground. Only his shoes could be seen, sticking out. A sigh of relief came over her. But with her nerves now slightly agitated, she decided to start heading home. Again, she heard footsteps.

"It's that hooligan again," she said to herself in a mutter, referring to the young boy.

But when she looked behind her, there was nobody there. The footsteps came from across the street. It was a man in a black hat and overcoat. Stephanie couldn't make out who it was in the dark. Soon, the man was walking alongside her from across the street. He never once looked at her, though Stephanie's eyes were on him the whole time. He started walking faster than her, and when he was ahead, he crossed the street. Stephanie slowed down her pace when she saw this. Why would he suddenly cross the street like that? she thought. Even more peculiar was the fact that he immediately started heading towards her. She didn't recognize him. She'd never seen him in her life. His nose and mouth were covered by a bandanna, so the only facial features that showed were his eyes. He was walking so fast that she expected he was going to pass her by like a comet. However, when he came within a few feet of her, he abruptly stopped. Not a muscle on him moved. A car drove by, and its headlights momentarily put a spotlight on him. Terror froze her to the bone. Those eyes! Those unmistakable eyes! She knew them! Knew them well! They were Bill's eyes!

Shaking her head, she took a step backwards. He took

one step forward. Her little dog started barking at the forbidding, shadowy figure standing before them. It was a sharp, high-pitched bark. Not very frightening. But it woke up several households and the lights went on in some of the surrounding homes.

"Come home with me, Steph," said Bill in a tone of urgency.

"I'm afraid that isn't possible..."

He pulled out a knife. "I'll slit your throat... and mine too, Steph. I'm not afraid. I'm not afraid to."

Stephanie picked up her dog and, mustering up a bit of courage, she blew past him, running as fast as her legs could take her.

"Stop, Stephanie! Stop!"

When she was at a safe distance, she looked back.

An angry neighbor came towards Bill. The neighbor didn't know him, but Stephanie saw that he had observed everything.

"Leave the poor girl alone, young man. You should know better than to approach girls you don't know in the middle of the night."

"Lick my boots!" Bill spat, making an obscene gesture before he got back into his car parked down the road and drove off.

Chapter 23

It took Flora less than a day to realize the harsh realities of life on the streets, and her thoughts turned more and more to John. Besides, she started to miss his comfortable spare bed, his kindness and generosity and, most of all, his interesting personality. She wasn't in love with him, but she felt herself very much drawn to him. To the person he was inside. He was a pure soul. Something she certainly wasn't. Therefore, she found him intriguing. Besides, begging was becoming more and more degrading to Flora. She came across nobody as generous or as friendly as John. At the end of the day, she could afford to buy only one meager meal. Hunger was her constant enemy.

"A word of advice, dear," said one elderly woman, holding rather tightly to her purse as she gave Flora fifty cents, "Go back to your mother and father. There are plenty of juvenile delinquents running around. You're opening yourself up, dear, you're opening yourself up to trouble."

Flora gave the woman a fake smile and roughly snatched the change out of her hand.

"Well, I never!" gasped the woman, backing away. "You ungrateful little slum-child!"

Flora had had enough. It was getting to be too much. She had never dreamed that life would be so tough and humiliating on the streets. But it was. And realizing how badly she needed John's help and companionship, she decided to pay him a surprise visit.

So many streets! She almost lost her way. Ah, there it is, she thought to herself, winding up at the little house.

When John opened the door, he looked overjoyed to see her. "No need to say a word," he said before she even had a chance to open her mouth. "I knew you'd be back. And I'm so glad you are. It's only been days since you left and you can't imagine how much I was already missing you."

He led her to the table and sat her down.

"I've made mashed potatoes and steak. There's enough for you."

Flora started eating like she'd just been fasting for a whole week.

"Poor child," said John, gazing at her sympathetically. "Yes, eat up now. You've been starving, haven't you?"

After the meal, she said earnestly: "I can't remember the last time I was this full. This is the best food I've had in months."

John was happy to hear it, and even happier to wait on her hand and foot. "Is there anything else you'd like?"

"No. Thanks."

"Then I'll prepare your bed for you."

"Oh, actually, if you don't mind, I'd like to take a quick bath." Flora knew there were foul odors coming from her unshaven armpits, and her vagina was turning red, puffy, blistery and yeasty-smelling; also, her breath was starting to smell because she hadn't been able to brush her teeth, and her hair was oily and messy from lack of combing and shampooing.

After her bath, she found John sitting in his bedroom, with a Bible open on his lap.

"What does it do for you?" she said, staring at the book.

"Reading the Word brings me closer to God, closer to understanding Him. It's about the closest thing to having an actual conversation with the Lord... well, besides prayer, of course."

Although Flora had always ignored the Marquis de Sade's radical ideas on God, Nature and Humanity, she couldn't have helped being affected at least in some way by his violent atheism.

"I have never been an enemy of God... but I don't think I've been his friend either."

"We're all friends of God," said John warmly. "Only good things come from Him. But He gets blamed for everything that happens, whether good or bad. It's time the Devil gets blamed for once."

"But hasn't Christianity been the cause of so much hypocrisy, bigotry, cruelty, fear and hatred for the last thousand years or so?"

"Yes... but only when people came along and twisted the Bible to suit their own personal beliefs and agendas. The Bible isn't corrupt to begin with. It's Good and Truth incarnate. But it's easy for evil or misled people to come along and use it to justify what they say and do. And then, unjustly, God gets a bad rap. Like everything else, even this book here in my hand, which is the greatest truth the world has ever known, which is the most precious thing in this whole world, this book too can be misused. And it's wrong. It's wrong."

"Oh, so all the evil and wrong done throughout history in the name of God have in actuality been the Devil's work? The Devil using 'corrupted' Christianity as a disguise to turn Humanity against God?"

"Precisely! That's right! How smart and perceptive you are! But again, I emphasize, the Bible isn't corrupt to begin with. It only becomes that way if we human beings twist its simple, true and literal meanings by allowing ourselves to be led by deception, or personal ambition, or greed, etc etc... The Bible, in itself, is infallible. It's the power of ultimate Good and Truth. There's a world of difference between orthodox Christianity and religious fanaticism. They're opposites."

Flora was persuaded. "I'll read it, then. If you'll let me... But God would never accept me. Some of the things I've done are much too horrible. No, there's no way he would accept me."

"Hard as it may be for you to believe, God's love is so great, so limitless, that he can forgive anything. Any crime. He is very merciful. That doesn't mean he doesn't want us to change our harmful and self-destructive ways, it means that we don't have to suffer guilt and self-hatred. We don't need our conscience to be destroyed by the feelings of shame. He releases us from that burden."

Flora opened her mouth, as if to release her own burden. But a moment of weakness and indecision stopped her. She was still too afraid to confess the sins of her past.

"Wrap your arms around me. I need to feel loved," she said, sitting beside John on the bed and embracing him.

He felt instant love for her. Not lust. But a deep sense of fatherly love. He was old enough to be her father – the warm, affectionate, open-minded father she never had.

But lust was an emotion that came far more easily to Flora, and before long, she found herself kissing his cheek, moving her lips over to his, and rubbing her body and legs against his, inching her fingers towards his crotch.

"No, Flora, no," he said, resisting gently but firmly. He wasn't angry with her, though. "We mustn't. I'm much too old for you. Our friendship is too precious to be shattered by a quick bout of sex. That's not the kind of relationship I want to have with you. I love you, Flora. I love you like a daughter. I want you to live here, with me. I have no one in this world."

"Neither do I," said Flora with a smile, tears streaking from her eyes. "We're perfect for each other."

That night, she threw her copies of de Sade into the garbage.

Chapter 24

Under John's moral and spiritual guidance, Flora started becoming a much better person. Purity grew in her soul with abundance. She atoned for her former wrongful deeds and her heart drew closer towards goodness every day, and with a hunger. It didn't take long for Flora to realize that, in actuality, she didn't want to be evil by nature after all. She had simply made the grave mistake of letting bad influences take control over her impressionable mind and rule her life. But that was all history to her now. She was making a new start. After genuinely giving herself over to Christ, she discovered a new peace, hope and happiness pouring into her life. Things were looking up.

"You're very special, Flora," John would say to her. "A more virtuous, more innocent girl there has never been. We're going to lead such a happy life together. Providence brought you to me. I'm perfectly convinced. Divine providence."

John took her to church with him. The well-spoken, powerful sermon was on the theme of the importance of reserving judgment and practicing tolerance towards those who we disagree with and those who veer off the straight and narrow path:

"People, whenever we see one of our own going astray," said the pastor, "let's not condemn, but instead, let's act fast and bring that brother or sister back on the right track, because the longer you wait, the harder it becomes for that person to break that temptation. We must be there for one another, both physically and spiritually. If we all look out for each other instead of just looking out for ourselves, everyone will be taken care of. This was the philosophy and lifestyle of the first Christians."

Flora especially liked the words he used to conclude the sermon: "I've often heard philosophers and politicians say that Humanity's greatest problem is stupidity, or deceit. But I tell you this: there is nothing more horrible in the world than when someone lacks sympathy, and the understanding that comes along with it. When someone doesn't know how to, or doesn't allow himself to feel pity, that person makes himself even more pitiful than that thing for which he feels no pity. Sensitivity to others is the single most important aspect of being human, of being humane; let's never forget that, even in a world as numb as ours."

After the services, Flora was introduced to a young woman her own age, named Lacey. She was a very upbeat, friendly girl, with big pretty eyes and a cute little smile.

"So you're Flora?"

"Ya. And you're…"

"Lacey."

"Say, that's such a lovely dress. I like the material," said Flora.

"Thanks. So, this is your first time coming here, right?"

"Ya, it is. I really like it, though. And I liked the sermon. It was full of emotion and it gave me that powerful sensation you feel when something bodes really true with you. You know?"

"Ya, I felt the same way… We have a young pastor. I like his energy, his profound understanding, and his modern approach… You seem real nice, Flora. I hope we can be friends, okay? All the young people here are really nice."

Lacey was a devout Christian who knew the Bible well, but she wasn't somber or reserved. Through her, Flora became acquainted with the other young people in the congregation, who openly welcomed her with warmth and enthusiasm.

When she and John got home that afternoon, Flora turned to face him. She had not said a word the whole time, she just kept smiling blissfully, her eyes fixed in a pensive gaze. With a meaningful-sounding sigh, she said, "Ah, that was the most emotionally uplifting experience of my life."

Chapter 25

When the sun came down, John and Flora decided to take a stroll through a nearby park. It was warm and pleasant outside. They had the whole place to themselves. Tranquility seized the air and everything seemed still and silent. Tiny stars glittered in the pitch-black expanse of space above.

"Did you really mean it when you said that any sin can be forgiven by God? And why does God have to be the forgiver?" asked Flora.

"When you commit an evil deed, you're not only wronging the other person or persons involved, but you're also wronging God because not only are you breaking the laws of the universe, but you're also going against God's nature. Most of us, whether we're Christian or not, want to do what God would have us do, which is, to do the right thing in any given situation or circumstance, but too often, we do the wrong thing. Why is that? Well, I have this theory. For a long time now I've felt that in each man and woman there is a 'dual' personality, a 'double' nature. What I mean by a double or dual personality or nature is that there is a good side and a bad side to each and every one of us. The good side we try to express, while the bad side we try to suppress. The good side is interested in doing the right thing, kindness, love, etc… while the bad is that set of instincts in us that display greed, lust, hate, and so on. For a person like myself, who believes in God, this is a very spiritual struggle – righteousness vs. evil, virtue vs. vice, divine nature vs. human nature. Like the philosopher, the scientist recognizes this struggle as well, the only difference being that he takes religion out of the picture. But either way, he's faced with the same struggle. And what a universal struggle it is! Personally, I like the Dr. Jekyll and Mr. Hyde metaphor from Robert L. Stevenson's classic. Our conscience tells us to be a good Jekyll, but our inner urges, desires, or whims make us do things we know aren't right or good, but they're attractive, enticing or beneficial to do, so we do them. Guilt and remorse follow. But we make the same mistakes over again, and this dulls our remorse... or we make new mistakes altogether! What makes the Mr. Hyde in us so powerful is that it has temptation on its side, a weapon it skillfully uses against us because it knows our weaknesses and preys upon them," said John.

"Do you, too, have this 'double' nature?"

"We all do. And as long as there is sin in the world, as long as we continue to live in an imperfect society, we'll never be able to shed the Hyde in us..."

They took a seat on a bench and John opened his Bible. "The Book of Romans describes this dilemma in clear terms. Ah, here it is," he said, finding the right page and verse. "And I'm quoting here: 'For what I want to do, I do not do, but what I hate I do... it is no longer I myself who do it, but it is sin living in me. I know that nothing good lives in me, that is, in my sinful nature. For I have the desire to do what is good, but I cannot carry it out. For what I do is not the good I want to do; no, the evil I do not want to do – this I keep on doing... For in my inner being, I delight in God's law; but I see another law at work in the members of my body, waging war against the law of my mind and making me a prisoner of the law of sin... So then, I myself in my mind am a servant to God's law, but in the sinful nature a slave to the law of sin.'"

This quote really spoke to Flora. It spoke to her so directly that she was stunned. All she could say was, "I fully agree."

They sat there close to each other, staring at the stars off in the distant night sky.

"But becoming a believer makes all your worries go away, doesn't it?" said Flora naively.

"No, Flora. Just because you're a believer doesn't mean there will be fewer problems, fewer temptations. God isn't an opiate, as once described by Karl Marx. And He doesn't show favoritism. God offers guidance and direction in your life, a kind of stability, a kind of hope and certainty. But he loves us all equally. In fact, God pours his love out most abundantly upon the wicked. When people asked Jesus why he spent his time with thieves and prostitutes and other disreputables, he said: 'do the healthy need a doctor? I have come because of the sick of this world.' He was speaking both literally AND figuratively."

"But what does God want from me, really?"

"All God wants is for you to acknowledge him as your Creator. Imagine a very loving mother giving birth to a child, and she's overjoyed by the birth, and she loves the child to pieces, but when the child reaches a certain age, he begins to question whether she in fact IS his mother. And thus, he rejects her. Imagine the pain that mother feels. That is the pain of God. That is the pain that God feels when the doubters and atheists of this world throw mud at Him, and laugh, and scoff. You ask what God wants from you? He simply wants you to put your trust in him; believing in him is the greatest extension of love you can show him. To love him in return one tenth as much as he loves you – even that would suffice."

They leaned back on the bench together and enjoyed the quiet and stillness of the atmosphere.

John mused, "Walt Whitman was right. How great it is when we realize how amazing and miraculous everything we take for granted really is. Take this starry sky, for instance. What a miracle! The only reason we don't view it as such is because it happens every night, or many nights at least. So the wonder of it fades away. But that doesn't make it any less of a phenomenon. Sunrise is another good example. Watching the sun come up and the dark suddenly disappear. Wow. And what a miracle it is to be alive. The one and only reason you were even born is because you just happened to be the first sperm cell to crack the 'egg' in your mother's womb. You won the race to the 'egg.' Hundreds of other sperm cells didn't, and they perished… It's food for thought, eh?"

Chapter 26

Now Stephanie was really in constant fear of her life – sometimes even paranoid. She wouldn't be left alone for one minute, either by day or night. In her mind, Bill was everywhere at all times. The first thing she did was to get a restraining order placed against him. He wasn't allowed to come within a one-hundred metre radius of her. The second thing she did was to file for a divorce.

When Bill was informed about what his wife had done, he collapsed into a violent fit. He was tossed into such hollow depths of despair that he literally hung on the verge of a mental breakdown.

"If it wasn't for that depraved, filthy whore of a sister, this would never have happened! Aaahh! I'll show her! I'll get her back for this!"

Getting one of his pistols from his wide assortment of hunting gear, he ran out into the streets, raving incoherently and shooting into the air.

"I'll get you, you little fucker! What kind of sick animal would entice her own brother! How perverted a mind must be just to conceive the idea!"

And to prove that he could never be seduced again, he stripped out of his clothes there in the middle of the street, with the eyes of multitudes on him. "Hear me now, people of this world," he announced, as if he were an alien from some other galaxy, "I stand naked before you now to make a point: nothing can stir my sex or its unclean

90

desires. I defy anyone to try and tempt me. I wash my hands clean of sex and sexual relations. Husbands, abandon your wives; wives, abandon your husbands! There's nothing but misery in love! It's a trap! Don't fall for it!"

Most people looked like they didn't know what to make of this glaring spectacle. He appeared and sounded like some lunatic from a previous century. Some laughed and joked, others were disgusted and disturbed, one or two even seemed indifferent.

Finally, somebody with a little sense took off his coat and tried to wrap it around the shivering nakedness of Bill. It was a cold day.

"No, damn you!" said Bill in a roar, "You're just trying to pacify me so you'll have me in a better position to tempt me, you fiend! I won't fall for it! I've built up my resolve! You won't tempt me, you, you..."

"But I only want to lend you my coat," said the man. It was none other than John Cooper, Flora's rescuer and provider.

"Okay... but one false move and I'll know you're trying to ass-fuck me!"

"I want to do nothing of the sort," said John. "Do you have a place?"

"Yes, I live alone in an apartment, over by the skating rink."

"May I offer you some food?"

Bill was returning to his normal self and he nodded. "I can't say I'd mind a nice, warm meal. Thank you, it's awfully kind of you."

For the whole time, Bill couldn't stop ranting about Flora, calling her every name in the book. However, he didn't actually say her name, referring to her only as "my bitch-goddess Lolita sister from hell." And many times he mentioned how she had confessed to him to the murder of Miss Strachey.

"Just wait till I find her! I'll have the cops on her ass before she can count to three!"

"Murder? That IS serious," said John. "I'll do anything I can in my power to help you see that justice is served. But how terrible a situation this is – to have to go against your own sibling. Only somebody with a strong sense of principle, a strong sense of right and wrong, and a strong sense of justice could do such a thing. And I commend you."

When they arrived at John's place, Flora was gone. John thought nothing of it. He recalled that she had told him she'd be going to the movie theater that evening.

Hanging up his coat, John pointed out casually, "There's a young girl living with me. I found her homeless and hungry on the streets, so I took her in some time ago. She's a great person. Really brought sunshine into my life. The both of us are as happy as can be."

"What's her name?" said Bill with a sort of suspicion.

"Flora."

Bill turned pale. "That's my sister's name! The one I've been telling you about!"

"No, it must be somebody else, calm down."

"No, of course, it must be her! She must have become homeless… after I kicked her out of my apartment. It's got to be her! Where is she, where is the slut? Has she tricked you into fucking her too, the little hussy?" He was sounding exactly like his father, Frank.

"Now calm down, calm down," repeated John. "You don't even know for sure if this is the same girl. Let's wait until she gets back. There's no sense in getting worked up over nothing."

"So she's clung on to you, eh? I'm not surprised. Not surprised in the least. You're a good man. She really knows how to pick 'em. She's a sly one."

John became very nervous, praying to God that his Flora wasn't the monster Bill had described.

As they waited for Flora's return, Bill, on the other hand, started feeling jealous of Flora's good fortune in finding someone like John and getting her life back in order. Besides, he wanted his revenge; in his heart he put all the blame on her for Stephanie's leaving and divorcing him. She ruined my life, he thought to himself, so I'll ruin hers.

It was a slow, silent and uncomfortable three hours before Flora suddenly arrived in the best of spirits. But when she saw Bill sitting across from John, there was a very obvious change in her mood.

"John, what's HE doing here?"

"Hello, Flora, my dear sweet sister," said Bill with a serene sarcasm that hardly concealed his ferocious hatred.

"This is your brother, Flora?" asked John slowly, as if afraid to face her reply.

"Y-yes… unfortunately. This is the asshole who left me for dead."

"Yes, that's true!" said Bill with vigor, "But only after you tried to steal me away from my wife. Well, it didn't work, did it? You may have recovered from the consequences of your action… but I sure haven't! And

93

never will! Stephanie's already started divorce proceedings against me! My life's turned into a living hell! All 'cause of you! You satisfied?"

Flora refused to speak, as if believing that the whole awful nightmare would end sooner if she didn't.

Bill continued by telling John all about the incestuous encounter, on top of repeating, "This is the girl who murdered her tutor, Miss Strachey, only four short years ago! She confessed it to me with her own lips!"

John was gripped by shock and disbelief, and he came to realize what a colossal error it had been on his part to get involved with Bill. If he hadn't offered him his coat in the first place, the present situation would have been avoided.

"John, don't listen to this lunatic! John, please, get him out of here!"

But John only sat there, totally lost in a daydream. He didn't know how to respond to any of it.

"Just come here and take a seat while I call the cops," said Bill, staring at Flora with fierce eyes.

"Do as he says," said John weakly.

After Bill told the police everything, the Strachey Murder File was immediately re-opened and Flora became their key suspect.

Within an hour, the cops would be taking her to the police department for questioning. After the reason for her arrest was specified and she was read her rights, one of the men in blue said: "You'll have to come with us."

"John, are you just going to stand there and let them do this to me?" said Flora when the officers cuffed her and started leading her out the front door.

John was in the midst of a deep and personal moral struggle. He couldn't think of what to say, so he said nothing to her. He stared down at the floor with wide and empty eyes. He didn't know if these new dreadful revelations about his 'daughter' had killed his love for her, or whether they were, in fact, even true. It was clear for anyone to see that he was going through more emotional pain and disillusionment than he had ever known. More emotional pain than he ever deserved. However, when he glanced up, Bill looked to him quite smug.

Chapter 27

The cop car raced down the empty streets. On that particular night, the streets were nearly deserted. Moonlight could easily be seen on the wet streets, for it had rained heavily the day before. In their hurry to get back to the station, the cop behind the wheel drove like a maniac. One sat beside him, while Flora sat handcuffed in the back-seat. The doors were locked.

The tires skidded after every turn. On one such skid, however, the car went over a puddle, which sent the whole thing spinning out of control. It crashed head-on into a tree, crushing and killing both officers in the front-seat.

Flora was unconscious for a few seconds, and when she came around, she started kicking at the window, trying to break it to get out. To her surprise, the whole door collapsed. She managed to crawl out of the car, but with difficulty. She had acquired several injuries from the collision. Her shoulder was out of joint, she had a fractured nose, and a piece of the shattered windshield glass had slashed across her forehead. Although she bled from nose and forehead, by far her worst pain came from her shoulder. She couldn't move her arm. It took only a moment to realize that she was possibly the only survivor. She looked around her. Nobody appeared to have been witness to the accident. Knowing that if she waited around for any amount of time people would soon be on the scene, she made a quick decision to escape. To flee.

Without another second to lose, Flora headed out of the city limits and westward towards the mountainous wilderness of the Great Rockies. There were only a few more streets and highways to pass before the nature she so loved encompassed her for the first time in ages. It was one of the very few things she felt nostalgic for when she thought back to life at the mansion. She paused, filling her lungs with the cool, crisp, heavenly air. In that moment of calmness, the impact of her situation really struck her for the first time. She was now on the run. Though only a suspect, she would be viewed as a convict just by reason of her escape attempt.

"Why did things have to turn out this way? I repented!"

She made her way into the woods, knowing full well that the only safe place for her would be the wild.

It didn't take long before the police car was discovered and an all-out manhunt was organized. They needed as many people as they could get. Helpful citizens were encouraged to take part. Everything and everybody was put on alert: 'A dangerous killer is on the loose.' Flora had several hours' headstart. Even though nobody had seen the actual car accident, it was immediately assumed that she had somehow been the cause of it:

"It was all part of her plan to escape," said the officer in charge to the mob of reporters. "She must have distracted the driver or God knows what. In any case, she must have done something. No officer would just crash his car... especially like this!"

So, new charges were filed against her.

There was a witness who testified, "My wife and I saw her running into the woods, towards the mountain range."

These were the very same mountains that could be seen from the pastures Flora had always visited as a young girl – the same pastures located not far from what was once her father's estate.

However, due to the encroaching darkness, the manhunt proved difficult, even for the tracking dogs, and it was soon called off and re-scheduled for daybreak the next morning.

Disgusted by Flora's escape and the police's inability to capture her that night, Bill became filled with more tension than he knew how to cope with. The time was an hour after midnight. His need to have Stephanie had never been so desperate. He decided this: either he would have her, or he would kill himself.

He drove up and parked on the street corner to the right side of Stephanie's house where his car wouldn't be seen because there were no windows on that side. He sneaked on over to their yard. The lights were all out in the house. He knew everyone was asleep. He also knew the inside well, since he'd been in it numerous times when Stephanie and he had been dating and she was living at home. He knew that the front door must for sure have been locked. But what about the backdoor? Bill was dressed all in black, like a burglar, like the time he confronted Stephanie with her dog on the sidewalk. His figure melded into the dancing shadows of the trees. With the stealth of a fox, he sneaked around to the back of the house.

What luck! he thought to himself, finding the backdoor unlocked. It led to the kitchen. Forgetting to close it behind him, he crossed through into the living room, his footprints staining the carpet, and made his way up the stairs. There was no mistake which was Stephanie's room – not to Bill. He hardly made a sound, twisting the doorknob with excruciating slowness. A slowness that seemed to him eons long. When the door was open wide, he was moved beyond comprehension. There she lay before him, like Sleeping Beauty, like the emblem of perfect grace, like a dreamy Aphrodite – his very own Stephanie.

Suddenly, the backdoor downstairs slammed shut on its own. It was a very loud slam. A draft did it. Since Stephanie's bedroom door was open, she could have heard it far more easily than her parents, and she stirred from her sleep, sitting up.

Fortunately for Bill, he had ducked down quickly under the bed and wasn't seen.

Finding her door open, Stephanie got out of bed to shut it, and just as she started closing it, Bill lunged at her from behind. She wasn't expecting it and was so totally startled that she fainted on the spot. She had a history of fainting, due to anemia and low blood pressure.

Bill scooped her up in his arms and carried her out the same route he had gotten in. By the time he'd carried her to his car, she was still unconscious.

A boy's voice called out to him: "Hey, you're that guy that was bothering this chick before! Whaddya do, liquor her up? You slime-ball!"

It was the same urchin boy who Stephanie had seen behind her the night she was walking her dog. This time, he was sober enough to stand on both feet. But that still didn't mean that there wasn't heroin in his veins or beer on his breath.

"If anybody's liquored up or drugged up, it's you! So

beat it, before I beat you into a coma!"

"Oh, I'm really scared," said the cheeky kid, snickering. "Is that what you did to her?"

If Bill didn't have Stephanie on his hands – literally! – he would have caught the boy and bloodied him up a bit. But he decided he had far more important things on his mind than childishness.

Laying Stephanie out gently in the back-seat, he wiped his brow, sighing: "This sure isn't what it's cracked up to be."

Ignoring the boy completely, he got into his car and sped away. He drove like a nervous wreck, accelerating through red lights, cutting people off on the road and nearly getting into at least three major accidents. Somehow or other, he managed to arrive at his apartment in one piece, in only a matter of minutes. Stephanie was still unconscious, or appeared to be, though she was slowly coming around.

He carried her out of the parking lot and into the apartment complex the same way he'd carried her out of her house and into his car. The superintendent just happened to be passing down the stairways.

"What's happened here?" he said. "Was it an accident... is she injured?"

"Oh, no," replied Bill with a cool composure that didn't come easy to him in any situation, let alone this one. "She fell asleep in the car and I didn't want to wake her, so I've decided to carry her to bed."

"I see. Well, good night."

Bill took her into the apartment and laid her out on what was once their bed. She stirred once or twice, but was still semi-unconscious. He bound, tied and gagged her, laying down beside her, resting peacefully, waiting for her to wake. It took only fifteen minutes. Stephanie lept from her position, springing up so fast it made her dizzy, and she fell back to the ground, bound like a wild animal. When she saw where she was and Bill standing before her, all she could do was panic. And panic she did.

"Help! I've been kidnapped! Somebody, help!" She tried to shout, but her voice didn't go louder than an inaudible murmur because of the gag.

Bill, meanwhile, looked like a man who just couldn't be happier. The broadest smile on his face represented his cruel delight in her useless struggle.

Suddenly, there was a sharp knock at the door.

A sweat broke over Bill's face. He began to panic almost as much as his captive. The TV was on, making it clear that he was home.

"Please open up, sir, this is the police… We only have a few questions to ask you, and then we'll be on our way… Hello? Hello!"

Bill realized that by remaining silent, he would only arouse suspicion. Leaving the bedroom, he carefully locked the door behind him and went to open the other door, confident that there was no risk.

"Come right in," he said cordially. "Would you fellas like anything –"

"No, no, thank you. And we're sorry to be bothering you this time of night. Generally we'd take you to the station for questioning, but since it's so late and what not, we'll do it here, if that's all right with you."

And they explained that they just wanted to question him about his sister, her possible motives for the murder of Miss Strachey, his relationship with her, etc, since he

101

was the one who'd turned her in to the authorities. The investigative officers were fully prepared for his answers – a pencil, note pad, everything.

Stephanie was finally exhausted enough to stop trying to break loose, and she heard the voices of Bill and the officers in the other room. This gave her new energy and she did the only thing she could think of to get their attention: bang the wall with her bound fists. This made a loud noise and the officers became distracted.

"What's that?"

Bill hesitated to respond and the officers burst into the room, knocking the door down to get it open.

One of them set Stephanie free. Bill made a run for it. But it was too late. The second officer got to him before he reached the apartment hallway.

Stephanie was returned to her parents before they even knew she was missing. As for Bill, he was taken to the police station and put behind bars until further notice.

"What, does crime run in the family blood or something? Holy fuck," said one of the arresting officers after Bill was securely behind bars in a holding cell. "First the girl… and now this individual, her brother. I'd hate to see how screwed up their father is."

Bill overheard the man and imagined what his father would have thought if he knew what his children had done to the family name.

The young urchin boy who had confronted him before was in the adjoining cell. He had been taken in for under-aged drinking.

"I knew they'd getcha!" he said to Bill.

Another man was sharing Bill's cell – a shabby,

drunken man with long, messed-up hair and filthy, smelly clothes. Bill couldn't come within a metre of him due to the horrible body odor. The drunk kept eyeing him. He was still tipsy, with the blank expression of an idiot.

"What ya think about morals?" he suddenly grumbled to Bill.

Bill looked away. Apparently he had nothing to say to this lowly tramp.

"I'm all for 'em, m'self," the tramp responded to his own question. "A little morality never hurt nobody… 'cept for, maybe, sluts or criminals… Criminals like us!"

"Shut up, shut up, you fool! I'm no criminal! I'm not a miserable, wretched criminal like you!"

The tramp burst out laughing. He couldn't stop. "On th' contr'ry, ma only crime's the drinkin'. But what you in here fer, eh? Ha, ha, ha!"

Chapter 28

The little orphan boy, Jamie, who Flora had abused years ago, was now twelve years of age and no longer an orphan. After his uncle had finally cleaned up his act, the courts had let Jamie live with him permanently.

Jamie was quietly eating his breakfast like on any other day the morning after Bill's arrest, when he happened to recognize Flora's picture on the front page cover of the newspaper. In it, she was being dubbed as the key suspect in the 1972 Strachey Murder, and the whole cop car accident story was inaccurately reported, further vilifying Flora's image.

"Uncle! Uncle!" exclaimed Jamie, so frantic and emotional that it looked like he was choking on a bone.

"What? What's the matter?" His uncle rushed into the kitchen. He was a real redneck, with his guttural voice, his body tough as wood, and his head just as thick.

The boy eagerly confessed for the first time his bizarre encounter with Flora, where and how it occurred, not leaving out a single detail.

"That's the girl who thrashed me!"

"Are you positive?"

"Ya. It's her. I never forgot."

If the charge of murder against Flora wasn't bad enough, a charge of child abuse was immediately added.

Chapter 29

The manhunt was resumed as soon as dawn brought with it the miracle of day, as Walt Whitman would have called it. Armed, the police and their volunteers separated into groups and headed into the murky woods to do the just thing. To do the right thing. They'd catch Flora and bring her to justice, whether dead or live. They were perfectly convinced of that.

Flora was deep in the wilderness. She awoke, raising her head up from the ground. It was a scorching day and she felt her lips very dry.

"What I wouldn't give for a glass of water," she muttered to herself. "Even a rainfall would do wonders."

Flora started to fear that she would become severely dehydrated. She'd heard of people dying from that condition. And she was feeling pretty light-headed, like she'd just guzzled a few glasses of gin. She touched the top of her head and it was burning like an oven. Her hair felt hot enough to catch on fire. She was sweating so much, she had a desire to be completely nude. Nude in some secluded pond that not even the animals knew about. Flora gazed at the sun as if mesmerized before looking away, momentarily blinded by the bright light and realizing what a pest it really was. When she had got back on her feet, walking brought back her stability, as she found shade in the density of the trees. She didn't know which way to go. Couldn't even remember from which direction she'd come the previous night, since it had been so dark.

Seeing that she was at the foot of a mountain, she instinctively began to climb. Never minding that she had no equipment with her, or anything else for that matter, her slightly delirious state convinced her that she needed to cross that particular slope, as if her freedom waited to be claimed just on the other side. Flora didn't think that her search for refuge in the wilderness was foolish or impractical. She didn't stop to think that she would soon be hungry, then hungrier, and then very hungry. She didn't bother to look that far ahead, taking everything one step at a time. Though in some ways very intelligent, she was still every bit the naive, over-idealistic nineteen-year-old.

In her effort to climb the slope, which continued to get steeper and steeper, she slipped several times, dirtying up her clothes and wiping away the sweat from her face with dirty hands. She never gave up, but tried harder when the effort was required. For the first time, really, she felt like a savage wanderer, an outcast of the wilderness, a child of the damned, homeless once again, and, like her brother, lamenting the fact that she didn't make peace with her father when there was still time.

"Spoiled little brat that I was!" she hissed at herself. "I curse the night I left the mansion!"

Late afternoon brought the relief of cloudy skies and Flora could finally breathe normally again, not feeling like she was being suffocated by the wafting heat. She could hear the flapping of wings, and when she looked up, there was an eagle hovering a few dozen feet above like some ancient Indian ghost that wouldn't leave her alone. It swooped down at her from time to time.

"Shoo! Shoo!" Flora waved her hands back and forth at the large bird, trying to scare it away. It was making her nervous and afraid.

She lost her balance and her foot started sliding. It wasn't long before Flora was rolling down the slope. Death looked to be just around the corner, as her tumbling out of control became faster and more reckless. Luckily for her, she was caught by a bush after only ten feet or so of descent. She gave out a loud scream. The parts of her body that hurt most were her injuries. Her arm started to ache like never before. She couldn't even touch it without shrieking in pain.

Finally she realized how pathetic her situation really was and a tear came trickling along the side of her nose, across her lips. She licked its bitter flavor, which tasted like despair. "I have no one to go to. No one to..." Then she remembered Miss Barrett. "If you hadn't left me, Tiffany, we could have been soaking up the rays on some Jamaican beach this very minute, with all of my father's millions in my grasp for both of us to enjoy," she sighed to herself.

But the daydream was cut short by her mind's return to the real world – not how things should have been, but how they really were. She began to ponder her crimes again, remembering what John had once told her: "Any sin, no matter how big, can be forgiven by God. That's how much He loves you. And forgiveness is important because it establishes reconciliation." Then and there, she felt a powerful urge to spit in the face of everything John had taught her. But she resisted the temptation. It would have been too easy. She couldn't just throw away like junk all those things she knew to be precious and true. But she deeply resented John's reaction to her situation, her plight. It filled her with grief. A feeling of total rejection – the absolute loss of the acceptance and love of someone she deeply cared about. She longed to be released from it.

"What am I even doing here!" she said aloud. "This is crazy."

Suddenly, the voices of men and the barking of dogs could be heard. Flora stayed in place, hidden behind the thick bush.

"We'll never find her in these wide-open spaces. My guess is she's already dead," one of the policemen said.

"How do ya figure?" another asked.

"Well, with all the wild animals – bears, cougars and whatever else, she can't possibly make it out here… Or else she'll starve. Either way, she's dead meat. Dead meat."

They were a party of six men, two of them armed. There were a hundred other groups just like them scouring the wilderness. The police officer who spoke last noticed part of Flora's shoe showing from out of the side of the bush and he alerted the others to it with his eyes. Flora had been watching and listening to them the whole time and when she saw them coming in her direction, she knew that they knew. And with the police having spotted her, and only a hundred or so metres away, she realized that she was caught. She realized the game was over. She could have kept running, but she was tired of running. Weak and weary with hunger, injury, and seemingly endless hours of difficult fleeing, she lacked the desire.

Flora stood up in perfect view of her pursuers and

slowly walked onto a cliff just twenty paces from the bush.

One of the men with a rifle aimed it at her, but the officer beside him yelled, "put that away!" The two men started arguing violently amongst themselves.

Flora paid little attention to any of it. As though in a hypnotic trance, she walked to the very edge of the cliff.

"I'm forgiven and clean now in the eyes of God... but still a dirty murderer in the eyes of mankind and the law..." Flora muttered. "It's true. When they catch me, I'm only gonna get what was coming to me. I'm only gonna get what I deserve. I know I deserve my punishment, I'm willing to accept it, and I pray, God, that you give me the strength to face it."

She prayed a fervent prayer, asking God to forgive all her wrongs and accept her as a child of Heaven.

She felt so pain-ridden, so alone, but this time there was no John to come along and invite her to his place for a succulent dinner. No John to offer his spare bed. No John to satisfy her emotional thirst for love and acceptance by enfolding her in his gentle, loving arms.

Lingering at the edge of the cliff for only a moment, she jumped off, to the shock and dismay of the six on-looking men. It was quite a fall, since she had already been halfway up that particular mountain-slope. She was dead before she hit the ground.

Chapter 30

Since the whole nightmare with the murder and everything else surfaced, John had been falling on a rapid descent, mentally. He stopped eating, stopped talking. He had to be taken to a hospital. His illness didn't pass; his great sorrow over the events prevented his recovery. He never left his bed. John continued to give everyone the silent treatment until he realized death was near. He could sense it, feel it.

From his deathbed, he spoke for the first time, stunning all those around him, for they had all assumed that he was deaf and dumb. These were his words: "How could I have abandoned you, dear Flora, right when you needed me the most? I was wrong! I should not have listened to your brother. It wasn't what God would have had me do. If Man's laws must make you pay for your sin, so be it... but I shouldn't have abandoned you, my dearest Flora. I shouldn't have. I should have stuck by you! I still love you! I love you more than ever, my sweet little girl!" Then, to everyone in the room: "Tell her. Tell her what I've just said. I want her to know. She must know!"

His face was red with emotion, the veins on his forehead nearly popping out. His eyes were wet and wide. In the middle of this agony and regret, he could sense the shadow of the valley of Death hover over him. Clinging to the hope of seeing Flora again in Heaven, he closed his eyes and expired, dying only minutes before he was to be notified of her tragic death.

Epilogue

The front page of the newspapers read: YOUNG MURDER SUSPECT DEAD. And there was a long, in-depth article about Flora, most of it biased against her, painting her as some horrible degenerate and criminal monster. At last, justice had been served, they claimed. The people back at Flora's church (especially Lacey) stood up for her alone, and they got a bad rap for it.

Eventually, Bill was tried and found guilty on charges of kidnapping Stephanie. He got two years in prison. When Stephanie heard the sentence, she said: "Two years? That's all?"

June 15 - July 4, 1996

Printed in the United Kingdom
by Lightning Source UK Ltd.
101410UKS00001B/282